University Foundation Study

Transferable Academic Skills Kit

Teacher's Book

Jane Brooks

Garnet
EDUCATION

University of
Reading

Published by
Garnet Publishing Ltd.
8 Southern Court
South Street
Reading RG1 4QS, UK

This edition first published 2007.

ISBN 978 1 85964 928 2

British Library Cataloguing-in-Publication Data
A catalogue record for this book is available from the British
Library.

Production

Project manager:	Rod Webb
Project consultant:	Fiona McGarry
Authors:	Amanda Fava-Verdé, Prue Griffiths, Anthony Manning, Clare Nukui, Andrew O'Cain, Frances Russell, Elisabeth Wilding
Additional writing:	Jennifer Book, Paul Harvey, Fiona McGarry, Lucy Norris, Ray de Witt
Editorial team:	Richard Peacock, Emily Clarke
Design:	Mike Hinks
Layout:	Bob House

Garnet Publishing and the authors of TASK would like to thank
the staff and students of the International Foundation
Programme at the University of Reading for their respective roles
in the development of these teaching materials.

Every effort has been made to trace the copyright holders and
we apologize in advance for any unintentional omission. We will
be happy to insert the appropriate acknowledgements in any
subsequent editions.

All website URLs provided in this publication were correct at the
time of printing. If any URL does not work, please contact your
tutor, who will help you find similar resources.

Contents

Introduction

What is TASK?

The Transferable Academic Skills Kit was written by English teachers and lecturers working on the University of Reading International Foundation Programme. It was produced to address problems faced by international students entering English-medium universities for the first time and to meet their needs. Originally produced as an online resource, the material was tested and adapted over several years. Its success means that it has now been published in book form. Consequently, the series has been developed and enhanced for a wider audience.

The first two modules explain the key skills and conventions that students need in order to be successful in higher education. The later modules raise awareness of and help develop a range of transferable academic skills. These include: organisational skills such as those involved in team work and exam preparation; conventions and skills involved in researching and writing essays and scientific reports; and skills needed for giving presentations and participating in seminars. There are also modules that help to raise awareness of skills needed for problem-solving and critical thinking.

Who is TASK for?

TASK is designed for international students at all levels, particularly those who are taking pre-sessional or foundation year courses. It is suitable for students studying a broad range of academic disciplines. The clear, step-by-step approach means that it is also suitable for students who have been studying in the British education system, but who need help in developing practical skills such as creating a spreadsheet, or who are unfamiliar with higher education conventions such as how to reference their work. The range of skills addressed is equally applicable to students studying at higher education institutions in Britain or in other countries around the world.

What do the modules consist of?

Each module is divided into six units. These are laid out clearly and consistently so that there is a logical progression to familiarise students with all aspects of the topic. Pictures and diagrams help to clarify concepts and stimulate ideas. The books are designed so that where written answers are required, they can be written directly onto the page.

Units contain tasks that help students with terminology and vocabulary, raise awareness of how theory relates to practice and provide practice in using key transferable skills. Exercises are carefully designed to build on previous work so that students can tackle more complex tasks as scaffolding is gradually removed.

At the end of each unit, there is a *Reflect* section that encourages learners to relate and reapply the skills studied in the unit to their own learning context, and transfer new skills to real-life situations.

Each module concludes with suggestions for extension activities and useful websites. There is also a glossary of high-frequency academic terms used in that module. The glossary can be used as an aide-memoire to remind students of the key terms in the book. It can also be used as a mini-dictionary.

If the series is used for class work, students should be encouraged to refer to the glossary when necessary and to select and record the lexis they will need for active use, e.g., categorising words in mind maps and tables. Teachers may use the glossary terms as the basis for additional vocabulary work and activities, e.g., gapfills, matching words and definitions.

How should TASK be used?

The TASK series is an extremely flexible learning resource. It can either be followed as a complete course, or individual modules can be selected according to students' specific needs. The materials can be used in taught classes or made available to students as self-access materials.

The activities involve using a range of skills and strategies, both spoken and written. They include the following: discussing opinions, cultural differences and questions in pairs and groups; reaching a consensus; planning written work and presentations; solving problems and evaluating different approaches; reading, analysing and evaluating texts, e.g., model essay answers or exam questions; making lists, completing tables and texts; correcting and reformulating texts, e.g., citing, quoting and reformulating the ideas of others.

Some modules also include collaborative practice and role play of academic situations, such as giving a presentation, taking specific roles in a teamwork situation and taking part in a seminar.

A number of exercises are designed to be completed in groups or pairs. The teacher may wish to focus on the oral work in class and set some of the written tasks for homework if time is limited.

If students are working independently outside the classroom environment, they should be encouraged to collaborate with other students for the purpose of such group work activities. Where student collaboration is desirable but unfeasible, due to the teaching and learning context, the tutor could work through group or pair activities with students during feedback and progress tutorials.

Students who progress confidently through the module can work independently to complete the Web Work and Extension Activities at the end of the module, whereas students who require additional support can work together with peers to complete these exercises.

Using the Teacher's Book

The TASK Teacher's Book provides answer keys and model solutions for the exercises and activities in each module. Where appropriate, suggestions are also made to assist with the logistics of classroom teaching, and additional follow-up ideas are suggested.

Key Foundation Skills

Unit 1 – What are transferable academic skills?

At the end of this unit students should:
- be able to identify key transferable skills;
- have a clear overview of the key skills explored in the *TASK* series.

Task 1 Identifying skills

1.1 Pairwork

The discussion could be initiated by asking the class to take an example of communication skills – reading – and to think about how they learnt to read in English. Did books in English look the same? Did they find information in English books in similar places to their L1 books, e.g., *title*, *contents page*, *index*? Which features were the same (transferable)? Which features were different?

1.2 Pairwork

Elicit the names of the occupations shown in the photos. Some possible answers might be:
   a) researcher/lawyer;
   b) salesperson;
   c) doctor/consultant/radiographer;
   d) receptionist/telephonist;
   e) site engineer/site foreman;
   f) hotel receptionist.

Set students to work in pairs, asking them to match a skill or skills with each occupation and explain why the skill is needed. It might be useful to get the class to focus on the photo taken on the building site and explain that problem-solving skills are important for a site engineer as things often do not go to plan.

If, when monitoring the class's work, you realise that they are still unclear about the meaning of 'transferable skills', it might be a good idea to conclude with a plenary discussion.

Task 2 Examining micro-skills

2.1 Individual work

Ask students to think about what the six modules might include, possibly jotting down keywords next to each module title.

2.2 Individual work

Give students a few minutes to read through the six module descriptions. They might find it useful to underline keywords in the module descriptions and compare these with their own ideas.

Answers:
   Module 1   f) Key Foundation Skills
   Module 2   b) Academic Culture
   Module 4   a) Team-Working
   Module 7   e) Introduction to IT Skills
   Module 10 d) Research and Referencing
   Module 12 c) Examination Technique

Ask students to compare their answers in pairs. At this point it may be useful to clarify the meaning and pronunciation of key academic vocabulary in the module descriptions, e.g., *lecturer*, *tutor*, *assignment*, *bibliography*, *quotation*.

2.3 Pairwork

Encourage students to reuse and paraphrase the key academic vocabulary in their explanations by getting them to imagine that they are talking to a child.

2.4 Pairwork

Ask students to think about what the six modules might include, jotting down keywords next to each module title. Ask students to compare their keywords in pairs and count how many identical keywords they have in their pair.

2.5 Individual work

Give students a few minutes to read through the six module descriptions. Students should compare answers with their partner. They might find it useful to underline keywords in the module descriptions and compare these with the keywords they had in common with their partner.

Answers:
Module 3 b) Seminars and Tutorials
Module 5 e) Problem-Solving
Module 6 a) Critical Thinking
Module 8 f) Essay Writing
Module 9 c) Scientific Writing
Module 11 d) Presentations

At this point it may be useful to ask students to use their dictionaries to look up the meaning and pronunciation of key academic vocabulary in the module descriptions, e.g., *objectivity*, *reasoning*, *bias*, *claims*. It is worthwhile pointing out that these words have a number of different meanings and so it is important that the students select the meaning of the word appropriate to the context in which they find it. 'Bias' in the Module 6 description is a good example to demonstrate with: a) the edge of a piece of material that is cut at an angle to the threads of the material b) an attitude that you have, which makes you treat someone or something in an unfair way.

2.6 Pairwork
Encourage students to reuse and paraphrase the key academic vocabulary in their explanations by getting them to imagine that they are talking to a child.

As an extension to this spoken activity you could ask students to choose ten keywords from the 12 module descriptions and write an explanation of each one for a child. Alternatively, you could ask them to write a description of the module they are most interested in, using their own words.

Unit 2 – Skills self-assessment

At the end of this unit students will:
- be able to identify their personality type;
- have greater insight into their personal learning strengths and weaknesses.

Task 1 Classifying personality types

1.1 Individual work
One possible introduction is to ask your students to focus on the group photo at the top of the page and elicit what the main students are like.

1.2 Pairwork
Encourage students to justify their answers by giving reasons.

Answers:
a) Jens   (4) methodical reasoner
b) Khalud   (2) practical realist
c) Hadi   (3) cautious thinker
d) Yuka   (1) action taker

1.3 Individual work/pairwork
Students could be given a choice of working mode here.

Task 2 Identifying your own personality and learning style

2.1 Pairwork
Encourage students to think about the implications of the figures for Theo's learning style, rather than stating the obvious. Depending on their level of English, you could encourage them to mitigate, e.g., *I think Theo might get a bit bored with thinking through the detail of an essay as he is so clearly an action taker*, or you could get them to hypothesise what it would be like to work in a group with Theo, e.g., *If we were working in a group together, I think I would trust Theo to brainstorm ideas at the start, but I probably wouldn't want him to be responsible for time management.*

2.2 Pairwork
Ask the students to jot down notes about their partners, particularly any examples or supporting evidence that is given to justify their self-analysis. These notes will be useful in the following activity. They should then draw a bar chart to represent the information they have learnt.

2.3 Classwork/larger group work
Ask each student to present his/her personality chart to the class or to a larger group. His/her partner should supply supporting evidence, e.g., *The reason Yoko sees herself mostly as a practical realist is that she doesn't like ideas for themselves. She likes to try them out by using them. Then she has a much better understanding of the ideas. She can see their strengths and weaknesses.*

Task 3 Understanding your strengths and weaknesses

One possible lead-in is to elicit some of the characteristics shown in the visuals. Encourage

students to use vocabulary from the box in Exercise 3.1 and use this as an opportunity to clarify meaning.

3.1 Individual work/pairwork/small group work
This is an open-ended exercise with no set answers. One possible extension of the exercise is to ask students to explain in writing why one characteristic might be both an advantage and a drawback in learning, giving examples from their own experience.

3.2 Individual work
Having completed the exercise individually, the students should compare their answers in pairs or small groups.

Possible answers are:

Learning Style	Strengths	Weaknesses
Action taker	adventurous, dynamic, imaginative	disorganised, unplanned, poor listener
Practical realist	pragmatic, logical	non-compromising, blunt and to the point
Cautious thinker	objective, careful, good listener	hesitant, unadventurous
Methodical reasoner	perfectionist, thorough	perfectionist, bossy

Tasks 4 & 5 Skills audit/Addressing your needs
The skills audit and needs analysis could usefully be done for homework and might form the basis for a tutorial with the students in your class.

Unit 3 – How organised are you?

At the end of this unit the students will be able to:
- identify factors involved in good organisation;
- analyse their organizational weaknesses and learn how to improve them.

Task 1 Organisation quiz

1.1 Individual work/pairwork
One lead-in would be to ask students which picture reminds them of themselves when they were younger.

The quiz could be done individually or in pairs. If you choose to let students do it in pairs, ask them to swap course books with their partners so that each student has the information about himself/herself.

1.2 Pairwork
Encourage students to ask each other questions, e.g., *How do you avoid losing things? What do you do in order to meet deadlines?* In a plenary session at the end of the task, you could elicit ideas for improving organisation. You could also ask students to reflect on how easy they would find it to implement these ideas.

Task 2 Targeting your weaknesses

2.1 Group work
Ask students to work individually to fill in the left-hand column of the table with their weaknesses. Then get the pairs of students who worked together on Task 1.2 to work in groups of, ideally, six to eight.

2.2 Pairwork
Ask students to re-form into appropriate pairs, on the basis of their priorities, with students from a different Task 2.1 group.

2.3 Plenary
Alternatively, this activity could be set as a written assignment for homework.

Task 3 Useful aids
One possible lead-in is to elicit which aids are low-tech and which are high-tech, using the pictures. Depending on the class, you could also ask the students which aids were available when their parents were at school, or which students own which aids.

3.1 Pairwork/small groups
It might be useful to elicit the vocabulary, using realia or pictures from a stationery catalogue.

3.2 Pairwork/pyramid discussion
Task 3.2 could be extended into a pyramid discussion by asking pairs and then groups of two pairs, etc., to agree which five items are the most useful. This would encourage your students to justify their opinions.

Unit 4 – Time management

At the end of this unit the students will be able to:
- identify factors involved in good time management;
- analyse their own time management skills and learn how to improve them.

Task 1 What is time management?

1.1 Pairwork
Encourage students to justify their answers.

1.2 Small group work
Encourage students to discuss the pitfalls of some of the statements, e.g., *Good time management isn't completing and submitting assignments as quickly as possible. If you do something in a hurry, it might be rubbish.*

A possible extension of this exercise would be to ask students to explain in writing why some of the statements about time management are misguided.

Task 2 Importance of time management

2.1 Individual work
Depending on the level of your class, you could use the information in the diagram to get students to write a few sentences speculating about their futures, e.g., *If I'm on time for class, I might understand better, but if I'm late for class, I might miss important information.*

2.2 Pairwork
It might be useful to revise the language for talking about similarities and differences. You could give your class some sentence heads to complete, e.g., *One thing we have in common is ...; Another thing we are both worried about is ...; You don't seem to be at all worried about ...; You don't share my worry about ...*

Task 3 Improve your time management

3.1 Individual work
This activity could be set for homework. In this case, Exercise 3.2 could be used to recycle language for talking about differences.

Academic Culture

Unit 1 – Understanding academic culture

At the end of this unit students will be able to:
• understand key terminology and concepts relating to academic culture.

Task 1 Defining academic culture

Lead in by asking students to choose one person in the photo and speculate about the identity of that person, what he/she is studying and how he/she is feeling.

1.1 Pairwork
As an extension to this exercise, students could be asked to arrange the keywords on a word map.

1.2 Pairwork
Answers:
1 beliefs (or attitudes)
2 attitudes (or beliefs)
3 culture
4 regulations
5 philosophy
6 research
7 thinking

For a lower-level group, it might be worth giving students two options to choose between for each item, e.g., 1 beliefs/study; 2 attitudes/research; 3 thinking/culture; 4 regulations/philosophy; 5 study/philosophy; 6 culture/research; 7 thinking/beliefs.

1.3 Pairwork/small group work
Encourage students to read through the definition again, identifying points of comparison, e.g., *beliefs, values and attitudes; rules for appropriate student behaviour; rules for appropriate teacher behaviour,* etc.

Task 2 Important words in academic culture

2.1 Plenary
Ask your students to identify what is happening in the photos and to say whether they have ever participated in a lecture/seminar/tutorial. If so, have they done so in English?

2.2 Individual work
Answers:
a) 6; b) 9; c) 4; d) 2; e) 1; f) 7; g) 8; h) 3; i) 5

2.3 Individual study/pairwork
Answers:
a) lecture
b) teaching assistant
c) plagiarism
d) personal tutor
e) summative assessment
f) further education
h) humanities
g) optional course
i) postgraduate

It might be worth mentioning to students that some UK universities use alternatives for terms such as teaching assistant (tutorial fellow).

2.4 Pairwork/small group work
A possible extension exercise to revise the vocabulary and for defining relative clauses might be to ask students to write definitions of five or six terms of their choice for homework, leaving out the term being defined. These definitions could then be given to another student to complete in a later class.

Unit 2 – The transition to higher education

At the end of this unit students will be able to:
• identify common challenges for students in the early stages of higher education,
• offer useful advice to these students.

Task 1 Identifying challenges

The purpose of this task is to allow students the freedom to talk about what has been difficult for them personally and to share this with other students who may have had similar problems. It may be that it is the non-academic aspects of the transition from secondary to tertiary education that have caused them most difficulty.

1.1 Small group work
Ask students to try and find more than one challenge for each photo.

Possible answers could be:
- a) making new friends/participating in teamwork activities
- b) organising one's own time/doing research/writing essays or reports/becoming an independent learner
- c) sitting exams/attending lectures
- d) adapting to living away from home/making new friends.

1.2 Individual work
Encourage students to add their own ideas about other challenges.

1.3 Pairwork/plenary
Students should be encouraged to give reasons.

Task 2 Offering advice

2.1 Individual work
Students follow the instructions in the course book.

2.2 Pairwork/small group work
This exercise offers the opportunity to revise language of similarity, difference and degree. You could give your students sentence heads to choose from, e.g., *The main difference between us is …; The two of us are as different as …; We are quite similar because both of us …*

2.3 Pairwork
Some students may enjoy doing this exercise as a role-play. Alternatively, it could be set as a piece of written work, with advice for each problem being written on separate pieces of paper. These could then form a wall display.

Possible answers could include:
- a) Identify slots in the timetable for self-study and timetable them in. Use a diary to note the deadlines for all assignments. Think about the process of producing the piece of written work. Break the process down into steps, e.g.,
  1 analyse the title;
  2 read around, making notes;
  3 plan;
  4 arrange a tutorial to discuss the plan;
  5 first draft;
  6 get feedback;
  7 second draft;
  8 proofread and estimate the amount of time needed for each step; then plan the time backwards from the deadline.
- b) Use the course reading material to help extend vocabulary. Keep a vocabulary notebook that includes information on meaning, pronunciation, collocation and grammar of words and phrases.
- c) Read module descriptions and the course handbook very carefully. Talk to tutors about course requirements and their expectations of your work. Ask other students if they can show you examples of 'successful' work.
- d) Prepare carefully for the seminar by reading recommended texts and reviewing lecture notes. Show that you are participating in the seminar, even if you feel too daunted to talk initially, by using active body language. Try and speak early on in the seminar. Make your tutor aware that you are having problems.

Task 3 Asking for help

Students' concerns may range from practical problems with opening a bank account and finding suitable accommodation to more complex ones, such as feeling homesick and encountering racism. To set the tone for this task, it might be useful to initiate the discussion by asking students to think about a time in the past when they shared a personal problem with a friend and to consider how they felt, how the friend reacted, whether the discussion had a successful outcome and what factors made the outcome successful or otherwise.

3.1 Small group work
Once the groups have identified several common issues, encourage them to think about appropriate ways of discussing the issue with a tutor.

3.2 Plenary
It might be worth mentioning the following points if they do not arise in your students' discussion.

a) It is a good idea to make an appointment with your tutor in advance, e.g., send an e-mail briefly outlining the problem and requesting a meeting.

b) It is important to recognise that the tutor is, in all likelihood, busy. This means that there may only be a minute or two for pleasantries at the beginning of the meeting, then the student needs to state the problem and give necessary background information straightaway.

c) The tutor might refer the student on to someone else. This does not necessarily mean the tutor is lazy or uninterested; it may be that the institution employs other specialists to deal with the type of problem the student is experiencing.

d) It is a good idea to thank the tutor for his or her time at the end of the meeting.

Such meetings cause many international students to be anxious. One possible extension of this exercise would be to ask your students to explore this type of tutor–student meeting through role-play.

Unit 3 – Expectations of higher education institutions

At the end of this unit students will:
• be more aware of expectations about teaching and learning in English-medium universities.

Task 1 General expectations

1.1 Individual work/pairwork
Lead in by focusing students on the visuals and then elicit what expectations are shown and why these expectations might be disappointed.

1.2 Individual work
Generalised answers might be:
a) D
b) F (Students should check past exam papers.)
c) T (In many institutions the pass mark is 40. A mark of 60 per cent or over is equal to a 2.1 degree.)
d) F
e) D
f) D (Students should check their student handbook and course handbook, but in most cases exams outweigh, or are of equal value to, coursework.)

g) T (In the UK, it is common for students to leave home in order to study at university.)
h) F (This would be unusual.)
i) T (Generally a register is taken.)
j) T (This requires marks of over 70 per cent and, generally speaking, only about the top ten per cent of students are likely to achieve a first.)

Students should be encouraged to check which of the above are true of their course at their future institution of study as there may be some variation.

Task 2 Expectations of lecturers

2.1 Pairwork
Ask students to use the visuals to give them ideas.

2.2 Pairwork
A lecturer would be expected to:
a) give lectures relevant to the subject – if the lectures are uninteresting to a student, maybe he or she is on the wrong course.
b) supply lecture handouts – these are often made available on the web in advance of the lecture.
e) set and mark assignments, though in some cases a teaching assistant may do the marking.
g) generally, lecturers know and use students' first names, but this can depend on the size of the class.
h) Generally this is true.

2.3 Individual work/pairwork/group work
Alternatively, this activity could be set as a written assignment for homework. Possible rewrites are as follows.

A lecturer would be expected to:
c) answer queries about content-related matters at the end of lectures, during seminars and possibly during a prearranged tutorial.
d) refuse to help a student correct his or her written English as this is not part of the lecturer's responsibilities; the lecturer might refer the student to the study/language support services within the institution.
f) take responsibility for a student's academic progress, but not for his or her social life.
i) supply a reference letter in support of a student's job/course application if requested to do so.

j) comply with the institution's rules and regulations governing deadlines. Generally speaking, lecturers do not have the power to change submission deadlines.

Task 3 Expectations of students

3.1 Pairwork
Encourage students to add their own ideas.

Students are expected to ...	Students are not expected to ...
• attend all lectures, seminars and tutorials; • let the lecturer know if they are going to be absent, preferably by e-mail; • take notes from the lecture; • read around the subject of the lecture; • participate in seminar discussions and answer questions; • give presentations; • use the library for research; • participate in group and teamwork activities.	• help the lecturer by cleaning the board or carrying books; • speak to a lecturer if they have a personal problem, although they can choose to; • join a university group or club, although it is advisable as it is a good way of making friends; • get a part-time job to help with finances, although this is very widespread nowadays; • buy small presents at the end of the term/semester to thank the lecturer, but it is a good idea to say thank you if you found the course interesting/enjoyable/useful, etc.

Unit 4 – Critical incident analysis

At the end of this unit students will:
• be more aware of differences between behaviour in their own cultural environment and the academic culture in which they are, or will be, studying;
• be better able to handle communication in potentially problematic situations.

Task 1 What is a critical incident?

Lead in by pointing out that, like much academic English vocabulary, the adjective 'critical' can have more than one meaning. Give the students some sentences to demonstrate possible differences in meaning, e.g.:

1 My tutor was <u>critical</u> of my argument and suggested I look for better evidence to support my view (i.e., expressing an opinion that something is bad).
2 The peace talks have entered a <u>critical</u> phase (i.e., difficult to handle as a small mistake might result in a much bigger problem).
3 After the car crash, his condition was <u>critical</u> for over a week. After this period, he was moved from intensive care into an ordinary ward (i.e., dangerously ill).

Then ask the group to read the definition of a 'critical incident' and decide which meaning of 'critical' is being used here (meaning 2 in the examples above).

1.1 Pairwork
If the students find this difficult, move swiftly on to Task 2.

Task 2 Reflecting on personal experience

2.1 Pairwork
Lead in by focusing students' attention on the photos and elicit what has happened in each picture and how each child feels.

2.2 Individual work
Focus students' attention on the photos and elicit what cultural features might give rise to misunderstandings.

2.3 Pairwork/plenary
In the plenary session it might be useful to ask students to predict which features might cause them problems.

2.4 Pairwork/plenary
Use the visuals to elicit some potential problems.

Generally speaking, answers would be:

Things you would do in a seminar	Things you would not do in a seminar
• use the tutor's first name; • disagree openly with other participants (but in a culturally appropriate way, e.g., *Yes, but …*).	• accept without question the instructions of a tutor; • make sarcastic comments during discussions; • wait to be asked before speaking.

The remaining two points would depend on a number of factors.

Asking to work with a different student from the one you were assigned to is a delicate matter. There might be circumstances in which this would be acceptable, e.g., the other student is unable to participate in the work, but has not informed the tutor. However, the students should try to resolve the matter between themselves where possible.

Agreeing with the general consensus even though you strongly disagree depends on many factors that might include the topic of debate and the gender and nationality of seminar participants. In these situations it is sometimes useful to verbalise what has shaped or informed our beliefs, e.g., *As a practising Christian, I believe that…*

Task 3 Critical incident analysis

3.1 Pairwork
Answers:
1. d) remembering to apologise at the end of the lecture and to give a suitable excuse
   a) might also be appropriate behaviour if a student is late for a seminar that involved a relatively small group of people
2. d) you can still see your parents in the evening
3. a) serious illness is usually considered mitigating circumstances if a student can provide a doctor's certificate
4. c) your tutor probably suspects you of collusion. This would be considered a serious problem.

3.2 Pairwork/small group work
The written part of this activity could be set for homework.

Unit 5 – Cross-cultural communication

At the end of this unit students will:
- be more aware of reciprocal speech styles common in English-language academic contexts;
- be better able to participate in academic situations such as seminars.

Task 1 Feeling at ease when you speak

1.1 Small group work
There are no right or wrong answers here as the question relates to your students' previous experience.

1.2 Small group work
b) is the most likely answer.

Your students might be interested to know that:
a) is reserved for a medical doctor.
c) is very formal.
d) is very informal.

1.3 Plenary
Some points to raise, if your students haven't already, might include:
a) If you do not know the lecturer at all, use his or her professional title (i.e., not Mr/Mrs/Ms/Miss) and family name.
b) If the lecturer asks you to call him/her by his/her first name, it is polite to do so.
c) Try to learn lecturers' full names early on in the course. Not using someone's name is considered impolite.

1.4 Pairwork
Answers:
a) T
b) F
c) T
d) T (in most cases)
e) T

Task 2 Reciprocal speech style

Focus students' attention on the visual and elicit how the different seminar participants shown are feeling.

2.1 Individual work

    1) b) (answer)

    2) c) (add)

    3) a) (ask)

It might be useful to have a plenary session at the end in which you elicit from the students that:

answer = agree or disagree with the question

add = make a claim and provide evidence

ask = either restate the question or ask a closely related question

2.2 Pairwork

There are no right or wrong answers here as the question relates to your students' previous experience.

Task 3 Giving yourself thinking time

3.1 Individual work/pairwork

Possible answers might be:

Techniques	Advantages and disadvantages
a) Pretend you haven't heard (picture 1)	Advantage: 'Sorry?' is easy to remember.
	Disadvantage: If you use it too often, everyone might think you are deaf.
b) Repeat the question (picture 2)	Advantage: It sounds natural.
	Disadvantage: You have to remember the question.
c) Use delaying noises (picture 3)	Advantage: These sound natural.
	Disadvantage: You can only use two or three, so they buy a little time only.
d) Begin speaking by saying, 'It depends ...' (picture 4)	Advantage: You don't have to commit to one opinion and you demonstrate that you can see more than one point of view.
	Disadvantage: You can only use this technique if you are being asked for an opinion.

3.2 Pairwork
Other suggestions might include:
Praising the questioner, e.g., *That's a really interesting question.*
Welcoming the question, e.g., *I hoped that you might ask me that.*
Promising to think about the question, e.g., *I'm really not sure. I would have to think about that one.*

Task 4 Applying discussion techniques

4.1 Individual work/pairwork
Instructions in course book.

4.2 & 4.3 Individual work/pairwork
Ask students to work individually on both exercises and then compare their answers with their partner.

Possible answers:
a) Do you think capital punishment is a good idea?
   1 (No) Mistakes are possible.
   (ii) Would it deter people from committing crimes?
b) Should we ban laboratory testing of cosmetics on animals?
   5 The decision should depend on what is best for society.
   (iv) What might the advantages and disadvantages be?
c) Is it a good idea for tuition fees to be free for all local university students?
   2 The financial implications would be very important?
   (v) Who would benefit?
d) Ought we to make it compulsory for all students to learn at least one foreign language?
   3 We need to consider who would gain what.
   (iii) How would this be determined?
e) Do you think the terminally ill should be allowed to end their own lives?
   4 (No) All life is sacred.
   (i) What about the consequences?

4.4 Small group work
It might be useful to get students to work in groups of three. Student A asks one of the a) – e) questions. Student B answers, using reciprocal speech style. Student C makes notes of Student B's turn in a table:
Is it a good idea for tuition fees to be free for all local students?

Answer	Add	Ask
It sounds like a great idea, especially if you are a local student, but I'm not sure it would work.	It would have huge financial implications for the government and non-local students might feel that it was a very unfair system.	What would the consequences be?

Students A, B and C then swap roles.

Alternatively, Student C could monitor the ways Student B buys time by completing a table.

4.5 Small group work
Instructions in course book.

Unit 6 – Philosophy of teaching and learning

At the end of this unit students will be more aware of:
• what constitutes good teaching;
• what is involved in learning a subject.

Task 1 A good teacher?

1.1 Pairwork
Focus the students' attention on the visuals and elicit which teacher the students think would be a good one and why. Then ask the students to broaden out their discussions to encompass their ideal teacher. Emphasise the need to justify their opinions.

1.2 Pairwork/small group work/plenary
Ask the students to work individually, ranking the characteristics. Then put them into pairs to explain their rankings.

The activity could be extended into a pyramid discussion, with pairs having to decide on their top three characteristics and then pairs of pairs doing the same, and so on until there is a whole-class discussion.

Alternatively, another extension might be to ask the students to explain their top three ranking characteristics in writing.
There are no set answers here as the students are asked to give their opinions. In the UK, characteristics of a good teacher would probably include a), g), j) and ideally i).

Task 2 The good student

2.1 Plenary
Focus the students on the visuals and elicit what activities the various students are engaged in and how these activities are good for study.

2.2 Pairwork/small group work/plenary
Ask the students to work individually, ranking the characteristics. Then put them into pairs to explain their rankings.

Like Task 1.2, the activity could be extended into a pyramid discussion, with pairs having to decide on their top three characteristics and then pairs of pairs doing the same, and so on until there is a whole-class discussion.

Alternatively, another extension might be to ask the students to explain their top three ranking characteristics in writing.

In the UK, b), c), e), f) and j) are generally assumed to be characteristics of a good student.

Task 3 Teacher–student contract

3.1 Pairwork
Ask students to take notes as they discuss with their partner, as they will be asked to report back to the whole class at the end of the exercise.

3.2 Individual
This activity could be set for homework. This work would form a useful basis for discussion in a tutorial.

It may be useful to point out to your students that UK universities tend to view their relationship with students as a contractual one. The idea of a teacher–student contract is therefore quite widespread and is an important aspect of UK academic culture.

Seminars and Tutorials

Unit 1 – About seminars and tutorials

At the end of this unit students will be able to:
- identify some of the key features of seminars and tutorials.

Task 1 What are seminars and tutorials?

Lead in by asking students to read through the introductory description and then decide which photo shows a tutorial and which shows a seminar.

1.1 Pairwork
Ask students to make brief notes on their discussion.

1.2 Individual/pairwork
Answers:
1. explore a topic
2. ideas and opinions
3. more informal setting
4. active listening
5. independent thinking skills
6. discriminate between facts and opinions
7. actively involved
8. ask questions
9. challenge ideas
10. supporting or conflicting evidence
11. learning experiences
12. discuss problems

For a lower-level group it might be worth giving students two options to choose from for each item, e.g., 1 explore a topic/discuss problems; 2 independent thinking skills/ideas and opinions; 3 more informal setting/supporting or conflicting evidence; 4 learning experiences/active listening; 5 discriminate between facts and opinions/independent thinking skills; 6 discriminate between facts and opinions/ learning experiences; 7 learning experiences/actively involved; 8 discriminate between facts and opinions/ask questions; 9 discuss problems/challenge ideas;

10 ideas and opinions/supporting or conflicting evidence; 11 ideas and opinions/independent thinking skills; 12 explore a topic/discuss problems.

Task 2 Key features

2.1 Pairwork/plenary
Ask your students to say whether they have ever participated in a seminar or tutorial. If so, have they done so in English?

a) How are seminars and tutorials different from lectures?

Tutorials and seminars	Lectures
• involve relatively small numbers of students; • are collaborative, with exchanges between all participants ideally; • students listen, formulate opinions, speak and take notes; • more freely structured, with participants developing ideas on the spot.	• may involve hundreds of students; • involve predominantly one-way; communication from lecturer to students; • students' main activity is to listen and take notes; • clearly structured in advance.

b) What do seminars generally aim to achieve?

Seminars are an opportunity to explore ideas collaboratively. Although seminars are group activities, they do not seek to establish consensus within the group (although this may happen); rather they give participants practice in using their own knowledge to develop and defend their arguments, communicating clearly and effectively and learning through teamwork.

c) How are seminars different from debates?

Seminars	Debates
• less structured • less confrontational	• more structured • more confrontational

d) What are the advantages of tutorials and seminars compared to lectures, self-study or distance learning?

Students can:
- ask questions;
- request clarification;
- show disagreement;
- get feedback from tutors and peers;
- develop team-working skills;
- learn from other students;
- discuss issues in more detail than in a lecture setting.

e) What kind of preparation might you need to do to take part in a seminar?
- attend a related lecture and take notes;
- read around the topic of the seminar, taking notes;
- consider what the key questions are in relation to the topic and make notes;
- prepare a seminar presentation.

f) What worries do you have as a student about participating in a seminar?

There are no set answers here. This question could form the basis of a writing activity in which students send letters outlining their main worry to an Agony Aunt partner who sends a reply providing advice.

Ideally, the questions should be discussed in a plenary session at the end of the exercise.

2.2 Individual work/pairwork

Encourage your students to jot down questions about aspects of seminars and tutorials they do not understand or are unsure about.

Possible skills are:
- listening to other people's opinions and evidence;
- sharing your ideas;
- dealing with conflicting viewpoints;
- asking questions;
- encouraging others to participate.

2.3 Individual study/pairwork/small group work

This activity often works well if students are given poster-sized paper to make a list of either DOs or DON'Ts for a wall display.

Some possible answers are:

Do ...	Don't ...
<ul><li>some background reading;</li><li>review related lecture notes;</li><li>listen actively;</li><li>join in the discussion;</li><li>ask questions (especially if you don't understand);</li><li>try to learn from other members of the group;</li><li>disagree politely;</li><li>be honest if you don't know the answer;</li><li>think about how the seminar is developing ideas in a general manner;</li><li>refer to previous scholarship.</li></ul>	<ul><li>expect others to do all the work;</li><li>remain silent;</li><li>be embarrassed;</li><li>sit back and use body language that shows lack of interest;</li><li>be negative about other participants;</li><li>take such detailed notes that you cannot participate effectively;</li><li>dominate the discussion;</li><li>make irrelevant contributions;</li><li>give an opinion without supporting it with evidence.</li></ul>

Unit 2 – What happens in seminars?

At the end of this unit students will:
• be familiar with some typical activities that take place in seminars.

Task 1 What exactly are seminars?

1.1 Plenary
Focus students' attention on the visuals and elicit what the people are doing in the various photos.

Possible answers to the questions posed:
What might you have to do in a seminar? *Give an individual or group presentation.*
What else can you do in a tutorial that you might not be able to do in a formal seminar? *Discuss problems (intellectual or personal) in more detail.*

1.2 Pairwork/small group work
Answers:

a)	L	f)	L
b)	S	g)	S/L
c)	T	h	L
d)	S	i)	T
e)	T	j)	L
k)	T		

1.3 Pairwork
As this exercise encourages personalisation there are no set answers.

Task 2 Getting the most out of a seminar

One possible lead-in is to focus students' attention on the visual and elicit what is wrong.

2.1 Individual work
Ask students to compare their answers in pairs or small groups.
Answers:

a)	T	e)	T
b)	T	f)	F
c)	F	g)	T
d)	T	h)	T

2.2 Pairwork/small group work
Encourage students to justify their opinions by explaining why a lecturer or tutor might respond positively or negatively to the different types of behaviour.

2.3 Individual work
This is another exercise where the answers are personal to the students.

2.4 Individual work/pairwork
In the pair discussions at the end of the activity, students should be encouraged to explain the problems that arise from their weaker skills. They should also be encouraged to prioritise which of the skills most urgently need work.

Students who:	Response of lecturer or tutor	Extra information
... are sometimes absent from seminars	negative	Students should inform tutors of absences in advance, ideally in writing, e.g., by e-mail.
... never participate	negative	The tutor might think the student is lazy.
... dominate a session	negative if other students want to speak; might react more positively if all the other students do not want to contribute	
... speak with an accent	neutral	Everyone speaks with an accent. If the speaker is clear, the accent is irrelevant.
... are good presenters	very positive	
... are very well dressed	neutral/negative	Dress codes for students and lecturers are often fairly informal.
... are frequently absent from seminars	very negative	Students should inform tutors of any major problems that are preventing them from attending.
... display their knowledge successfully	positive	As long as this is for the purpose of exploring a topic.
... ask questions	very positive	Questions are often a sign of active thinking.
... are happy to collaborate with other students	very positive	
... do not finish assignments on time	negative	If the student cannot give a presentation, he/she should contact the tutor as soon as possible so that the tutor can plan an alternative.

Unit 3 – Subject knowledge

At the end of this unit the students will be able to:
* plan input and prepare for a seminar more effectively.

Task 1 Preparing for a seminar

1.1 Individual work/plenary
Answers:

a)	T	e)	?
b)	P	f)	?
c)	?	g)	P
d)	P	h)	F

Task 2 Thinking about, researching and discussing issues

Ask students to look at the visual. Elicit the topic of the seminar. Ask students to work in pairs, sharing any information they already know about the topic of cloning or the case of Dolly the sheep. Then have a brief plenary session, collecting ideas on the board.

2.1 Individual work/pairwork/small group work/plenary
Ask students to work in pairs on analysing the topic and the main issues involved. In a plenary session, elicit what the main positions are on this issue and add this information to the ideas already on the board. Encourage students to make notes, as these notes will form the basis of a further activity (Exercises 3.2 & 3.3).

Divide students into AA and BB pairs. Ask 'A' students to read the first two definitions, underlining important information. Ask 'B' students to do the same with the third and fourth definitions. 'A' students should work in their pairs to clarify meaning and check the important information in definitions one and two. 'B' students should also work in their pairs, carrying out the same activities for definitions three and four. Information can then be exchanged in either AB pairs or in AABB small groups.

A possible extension activity would be to ask students to make notes on all four definitions. This could be done for homework and this work could then form the basis for a note-taking comparison focusing on content, style, layout, bibliographical details, etc.

2.2 Individual work/pairwork
Some of your students may be unfamiliar with de Bono's PMI method. If this is the case, elicit if the following points are Plus points (P), Minus points (M) or Interesting points (I).

* Cloning is a naturally occurring process, e.g., identical twins. (P)
* 'S/he is a complete clone' has a negative connotation in many cultures, particularly those that value originality and individuality. (I)
* Cloning is meddling with nature. (M)

Ask students to brainstorm individually and then share their ideas with a partner. Alternatively, the brainstorming could be done for homework.

2.3 Individual work
This individual research task could be used to prepare an information exchange activity in a later class if students are assigned one of the three texts to read and make notes on.

Students should also be encouraged to identify at least one other source on this topic and take notes on it in preparation for an information exchange session in class.

Task 3 Establishing and supporting your opinion

3.1 Individual work
Encourage students to develop one point in the three sentences, giving an opinion and supporting points and/or evidence.

3.2 Individual work
Remind the students of the issues the class identified in Exercise 2.1. Ask students to check that they have addressed (some of) the issues identified by the class. Ask them to redraft their texts if necessary.

3.3 Small group work

Ask students to read their texts aloud to their group members and discuss any changes they made after they had checked their work against the issues they had previously identified.

3.4 Individual work

Depending on the level of your students, it may be necessary to pre-teach the following:

- diversity
- adaptability
- a species
- to wipe something out
- Black Death

Ask students to read the text about the potential threat posed by a loss of diversity and underline in different colours the writer's viewpoint, explanations, the effect of cloning and evidence. After students have compared their answers in pairs, they should complete the table.

Argument/ issue	For/against	Explanation	Effect	Evidence
cloning would reduce biodiversity	against cloning	clones are genetically identical to the parent organism so lack diversity	survival will be threatened if organisms have less diversity	biological diversity prevented species from being wiped out in past

3.5 Individual work/small group work

This could be set for homework. Alternatively, if the research task in Exercise 2.3 was set up with students being assigned one source text only, students could now work in groups of three, exchanging ideas and information.

If students were required to identify their own sources in Exercise 2.3, they could now work in small groups and exchange the ideas and information they discovered.

Students' answers will vary, but might include the following points:

For:
Cloning could ...

- help people live longer;
- help people with incurable diseases;
- save endangered species;
- help infertile couples have children.

Against:
Cloning could ...

- be unethical;
- decrease genetic diversity;
- threaten people's individuality by reducing them to manufactured products.

Unit 4 – The language of seminars and tutorials

At the end of this unit students will:

- have developed a range of communication skills and strategies to help them take part effectively in group discussions.

Task 1 Useful language for contributing to group discussions

1.1 Pairwork
Follow course book instructions. Answers will vary from student to student.

1.2 Pairwork
Select one expression from each category. Write one of the expressions on the board and ask students to match it with one of the eight categories, and so on. This would allow students to ask for clarification about the different categories.

The students could then be asked to work in pairs and put the remaining expressions in the appropriate categories. Other alternatives are:

1 Put the students in AB pairs. Student A dictates the expressions to Student B, who writes them in the correct category.
2 The phrases are copied onto strips of paper that are then stuck on the wall. AB pairs do a running dictation, with Student A running across the classroom to the strips, memorising the phrase, running back to Student B, who writes down the expressions on strips. A and B could swap roles half-way through. The AB pair could then put the expressions into the eight categories.

Answers:

Asking questions in seminars and group discussions
1 Asking a question m) I have a question about X. p) I would like to ask you something about X.
2 Asking for repetition when you haven't heard what has been said f) I didn't quite catch that … o) Could you repeat that please?
3 Asking for clarification when you haven't completely understood the message d) Could you explain what you meant when you said that …? h) I'm afraid I didn't follow your point about …   Could you go over that again? k) Could you go over what you said about …? v) Can I check that I've understood?
4 Asking someone to be more specific b) If I might interrupt for a moment … g) Excuse me … i) You mentioned X …

Stating opinions and summarising
1 Disagreeing with what has been said j) I see what you mean, but … q) You have a point there, but … r) I'm afraid I don't agree with that. t) Certainly it's true that … but on the other hand …
2 Adding something to what has been said a) I'd just like to add …
3 Agreeing with what has been said c) X put it very well when he/she said … u) I fully agree with X …
4 Summarising what has been said e) On balance … l) Overall … n) To sum up … s) X raised some important points.

Task 2 Communication strategies in context

2.1 Pairwork
Ask students to work in pairs on this exercise.

Possible answers include:
a) Sorry, I didn't quite catch that …
   Sorry, could you repeat that please?
b) Sorry, could you explain what you mean by X?
   Sorry, what does X mean?
c) I have a question about X.
   What/When/How/Who/Where …?
   I would like to ask you something about X.
   What/When/How/Who/Where …?
d) I scc what you mcan, but …
   You have a point there, but …
   I'm afraid I don't agree with that.
   Certainly it's true that … but on the other hand …
e) X put it very well when he/she said…I'd just like to add that …
   I fully agree with X … I'd just like to add that …
f) If I might interrupt for a moment?
   I don't want to interrupt, but I'd like to add that …
g) On balance …
   Overall …
   To sum up …
   X raised some important points.
h) I'm afraid I didn't follow the point about …
   Could you go over that again?
   Could you go over what was said about …?
i) I'm not sure I've completely understood the text. Could you summarise the main ideas please?

Task 3 Practise using communication strategies

Lead in by asking students to speculate about which issues are represented in the visuals.

3.1 Pairwork/small group work
Possible ways of organising this task, depending on the resources available, are:

1 For students who like cooperating – record the students discussing the questions in pairs and then ask the pair to listen to their work, making a note of which expressions from Task 2 they used.

2 For students who enjoy competing – put the target expressions from Task 2 on separate pieces of card. Get students to work in groups of three to divide the expressions up equally among themselves and to place the cards on the desk in front of them, language-side up, so it is clear whose expressions are whose. Ask the groups to discuss one of the issues in the course book. They

should try to incorporate expressions on the other students' cards. Each time they manage to do this they should take the appropriate card from the other student. Stop the activity after three minutes and ask students to count the number of cards they have. Ask the students to fill in the relevant part of the table in Exercise 3.2 from memory. Then ask students to move on to the next issue.

3.2 Pairwork/small group work
If you used Method 1 above, ask each pair to listen to their recording and fill in the table. This could be done for homework.

If you used Method 2 above, Exercise 3.2 was integrated into Exercise 3.1.

Task 4 Language activation

4.1 Individual work/pairwork/plenary
This review could be done individually, with students trying to remember one expression for each situation. Alternatively, in AB pairs, Student A could give a language function from the list in the course book, e.g., *agree*. Student B responds with one example expression. As another alternative, the group could work as a whole. Student A throws a ball to Student B and names a category from the list. Student B catches the ball, responds with one example expression and throws a ball to Student C, naming another category from the list.

4.2 & 4.3 Small groups
See the instructions in course book. Your role here is to monitor and offer feedback in a plenary session at the end of the activity.

Unit 5 – Participation

At the end of this unit students will:
• have developed and practised some communication strategies for seminar and tutorial participation.

Task 1 Getting involved

1.1 Individual work/pairwork/small group work
This exercise could be set as homework to be prepared before the class. Alternatively, students could work through the personalisation stage individually. (Have you done these activities before?)

You might need to model an answer to the first activity for the second question, What skills does each activity involve?, i.e., *after a lecture, following up some questions and preparing answers:*

This involves reading through my lecture notes and making a note of any questions that remain unanswered or I am not clear about. I then need to do research, either in the library or using the Internet, and find relevant sources. Then I need to locate relevant sections in the source as fast as possible and take notes. If my research raises any other questions, I need to jot them down so that I can raise them in a seminar or tutorial.

1.2 Large group work
The organisation of this task depends on the needs and interests of your class. If all the students are going to study a similar subject you might want to organise the students into groups of ten. If your students are going on to study a number of different subjects, they might like to organise themselves into smaller groups of related subjects.

Task 2 More preparation: Roles and stages

2.1 Individual work/pairwork
Possible answers are:
  a) Ask an individual student – 3, 4, 5, 6, 7, 8, 9, 10, 11
  b) Paraphrase – 1, 3
  c) Summarise – 1, 3, 4, 7, 8
  d) Ask for – 6, 10, 11
  e) Thank – 5
  f) Introduce – 1, 2, 3
  g) Outline – 1, 3, 8
  h) Provide – 4, 6, 10, 11

It might be useful to have a plenary session at the end in which you compare answers to the exercise as a class and elicit other ideas from the students. Other ideas might include: a) encouraging others to speak; b) making sure people have time to think and answer; c) listening actively; d) respecting all opinions.

2.2 Pairwork/small group work/plenary
Possible answers are:

Yes	No
2, 5, 6, 7, 9, 10, 14, 16	1, 3, 4, 8, 11, 12, 13, 15

Task 3 Seminar role play

3.1 Group work
If possible, record the students' seminar(s) so that they can review their performance before moving on to Task 4.

Task 4 What kind of contributor am I?

4.1 Pairwork/small group work
Students' answers will vary. One possible extension is for students to write up a set of objectives for their next seminar.

4.2 Individual work/pairwork/small group work/plenary
Answers to the first task will vary from student to student. The second task lends itself to a pyramid discussion.

Unit 6 – Different types of seminars and tutorials

At the end of this unit students will:
- be more aware of the different types of seminars and tutorials in which they might participate in higher education.

Task 1 Seminar and tutorial activities

1.1 Individual work
Possible answers are:

Activity	Before	During
b) You present a paper	Research the topic and take notes; select and organise your material; write notes; prepare visual aids; predict the questions you will be asked; prepare answers and practise.	Present clearly from notes; use visual aids; thank the audience for listening and answer questions.
c) Another student presents a paper	Research the topic; make notes and prepare questions.	Listen actively; take notes; thank the speaker and ask questions.
d) A guest speaker gives a talk followed by discussion	Research the topic; find out information about the speaker; prepare questions.	Listen actively; take notes; thank the speaker and ask questions.
e) You give an informal presentation with several other students	Divide up the tasks noted in 1 between the group and arrange to practise as a group.	Present clearly from notes; use visual aids; thank the audience for listening and answer questions.
f) You read a text during the seminar and discuss the topic	Read around the topic and review lecture notes.	Find key ideas in the text; analyse the argument; listen to others; give opinions; agree and disagree; take brief notes.
g) You lead a seminar	Research the topic; make notes; prepare an overview of the issue.	Give an overview of the topic; elicit and value the opinions of others; take brief notes; manage time; summarise the main ideas and thank everyone for taking part.

Students should compare ideas with a partner. Encourage students to think about advice they could give to their partners regarding the activities they find hard.

1.2 Pairwork
Ask the students to discuss other activities they might do in a tutorial.

Possible answers to complete the list include: a) you receive feedback on a piece of writing; b) you ask advice about sources of information or an exam; c) you receive feedback on your overall progress.

1.3 Individual work/pairwork
Possible answers include:

Activity	Before	During
a) You, a tutor and two other students discuss a topic	Research the topic; take notes and prepare questions.	Listen actively; give opinions; agree; disagree; take notes and thank everyone.
b) A tutor helps you, on your own, to prepare a piece of writing	Research the topic; make notes; write a plan of the essay and prepare questions.	Listen actively; explain your ideas clearly; take notes; ask questions and thank the tutor.
c) You go and see a tutor about a personal problem	Arrange an appointment; plan what information you need to share with your tutor.	Speak succinctly; listen actively; evaluate the advice and thank the tutor.

Encourage students to think about advice they could give to their partners regarding the activities they find hard.

Task 2 Example activity: Giving a presentation

2.1 Individual work
Possible answers might include:
- When planning and selecting material, think about the audience's needs and the time available.
- Find evidence to support your points.
- Organise the material into a clear structure.
- Prepare effective visual aids and handouts.
- Write notes on cards attached together.

- Practise pronouncing key words clearly.
- Practise once yourself and once with a friend.
- Identify any technical terms unknown to your audience and explain them simply.
- Repeat key ideas.
- Maintain good eye contact with the audience.
- Stay calm if a problem occurs.

2.2 Individual work/pairwork/small group work
Possible answers might include:

Yes	No
2, 5, 6, 7, 9, 10, 14, 16	1, 3, 4, 8, 11, 12, 13, 15

Task 3 Example activity: Personal tutorials

3.1 Individual work/pairwork
One possible lead-in is to elicit from students background information about their previous experience of tutorials, e.g., *Have you had tutorials before? When? Where? With whom? How long did they last?*

Possible answers (point out to students that tutorials will differ from university to university and tutor to tutor, so the answers are very general guidelines):
   a) More than once a term.
   b) Compulsory, particularly at the beginning of the course.
   c) Depends on students' experiences.
   d) You need a balance between you and your tutor.

3.2 Individual work/pairwork
Possible answers might include:
- Confront the bully.
- Find out why you cheated/plagiarised and remedy the problem.
- Take appropriate action; get a medical certificate to prove illness.
- Analyse and address the cause of poor attendance.
- Be clear about what help you want; prioritise your questions as the tutor is likely to be busy.
- Prepare your questions and prioritise them; take any evidence of mitigating circumstances if you have had problems.
- Talk to the lecturer concerned first; use appropriate indirect language; be clear about what your complaint is.

Team-Working

Unit 1 – Teamwork in action

At the end of this unit students will:

- understand key considerations when working in teams;
- be more aware of how team-working involves and develops different skills.

Task 1 Factors to consider when working as a team

Lead in by asking students to read through Robbins's definition of a team individually. Then ask half the class to work in small groups to discuss the quotation's meaning and the other half to think about its meaning individually. After a plenary session about the meaning of the quotation, there would be a natural link into the first question in Exercise 1.1.

1.1 Pairwork
Ask students to make brief notes on their discussion.

Possible answers might be:
- a) Student's own preference.
- b) Generally speaking, an increasing amount of emphasis is being placed on teamwork in UK higher education institutions and in many workplace settings.
- c) Be prepared to compromise; exploit team members' strengths to achieve the team's goal; avoid dominating or imposing your own views.

1.2 Small group work
Some possible answers:
- a) Play football, basketball, cricket.
- b) Achieve goals at work, e.g., plan a sales campaign.
- c) Sing in a choir or play in a musical group/band.

It can be useful/necessary to work in teams because:

- a) the activity cannot happen without team-working, e.g., game of football;
- b) the group has a skills mix that no individual could have;
- c) mutual support among the team members achieves a better result than might otherwise have been obtained;
- d) the interaction between team members achieves a better result than might otherwise have been obtained.

Task 2 Do a teamwork activity

2.1 Small group work
The instructions for this activity are given in the course book. Below is a small version of a photocopiable sheet (see page 34) for the observers.

OBSERVER'S SHEET
Your task is to watch the group at work and think about how well, or not, they work together. To help you do this, make brief notes in the spaces below. As you need to give feedback on the team's ability to manage its time, you need to be able to see a clock, watch or mobile phone. At the end of the 20-minute period, stop the team's activity and mark its work.

Questions	Observer's comments
Did all the members of the group contribute or did some members dominate?	
What were the team's strengths and weaknesses?	
What techniques did they use to solve the problems?	
How well did the team keep to time?	
What was the team's score?	

Answers:
a) Ten.
b) The letter 'r'.
c) The first men – three sacks of corn are heavier than three empty sacks.
d) It was a ground floor window.
e) Three minutes. The pan is large enough to cook them all together.
f) The coin in bucket A – ten degrees Fahrenheit is below freezing, so the coin will just sit on the ice.
g) Neither. If something is cut in half, both halves are the same size.
h) She was returning home on foot.
i) At one minute before the hour.
j) Yes – "'I' is the 9th letter of the alphabet."
k) Being the youngest person in the world.
l) None – pages 33 and 34 are always two sides of the same leaf.
m) Three – each sock could either be red or blue, so even if the first two socks are different colours, the third will have to match one or the other.
n) Ten.
o) All haystacks together = one large pile.
p) Friday (=fry), Tuesday (= choose), Wednesday (= wed), Sunday (= sunny)

DEBRIEFING SESSION

In the debriefing session you should make a number of comments, both positive and negative. It is important to practise using indirect language when you make critical comments:

Avoid saying …	Use indirect language …
You talk too much.	It is important to listen to the others as well as expressing your own ideas.
You didn't say anything.	Perhaps you could try to contribute a bit more to the discussion.
You weren't interested in other people's ideas.	Your ideas are valuable as are other people's. Perhaps you could have been more open to theirs?
You avoid eye contact with others.	You made some good points but they could have had more impact if you had used more eye contact.

2.2 Plenary

When the exercise is over, the observers feed back to the group initially. The team members should be encouraged to listen carefully to their observer's comments and to evaluate them as a team, before responding to the observer.

This debrief session should then be opened up to the whole class. Although the discussion is student-led, the teacher could collect on the board the ideas that emerge, using the same framework as that provided for the observers.

Task 3 What have you learned about roles and teamwork?

3.1 Small group work

Ask each group to choose one of the situations listed and then think about different roles that would be necessary to complete the task. Once the group has agreed on these, ask the members of the group to work individually, allocating specific roles to individuals in the team. When this stage has been completed, the students should compare their ideas, giving reasons for their choices, e.g.:

I think Khaled should be the time manager for this project as he did such a fantastic job of moving us on in the last teamwork activity.

I think Jingjing should be responsible for interviewing members of the public about their preferences as she is so good at putting people at their ease.

3.2 Small group work

Possible answers might be:
a) You should value everyone's contributions.
b) You should try to put yourself into other team members' shoes to understand their points of view.
c) You should all try to resolve conflicts that arise between team members.
d) You should trust each other to fulfil their roles, but be prepared to help if someone needs a hand.
e) You should thank other team members for their contributions.

This session could be concluded by asking the group what was the single most important thing they learnt about themselves or teamwork from the lesson.

In preparation for the next lesson, students could be asked to work in groups of three and agree upon a talented individual they admire, e.g., a film star, a musician or a politician. If possible, they should find a picture of the person and fill in the grid given in Unit 2, Exercise 1.1. The group could then prepare a mini-presentation to give to another group within the class (Unit 2, Exercise 1.2).

Unit 2 – Why teamwork?

At the end of this unit students will:
• be more aware of the benefits and potential problems of working in a team.

Special materials
Bring in some everyday objects, e.g., mug; sunglasses; keys.

Task 1 What are the benefits of teamwork?

1.1, 1.2 & 1.3 Small group work
Answers depend on whom the groups choose, as this task is student-led. The teacher's role is that of dropping in and out of the various groups' discussions, possibly helping students to make connections between individuals and teams.

After Exercise 1.3 has been discussed within the pairs of small groups, the discussion could be opened out. The pairs of small groups could be asked to report their findings, which are collected on the board. Allow ten minutes for this feedback session.

Task 2 What are the problems of teamwork?

One possible lead-in is to focus students' attention on the visual and elicit what is wrong.

2.1, 2.2 & 2.3 Small group work
Ask students to go back to working in their small groups and complete the first activity, making notes in the grid. Pairs of groups should then share their ideas, before discussing the advantages and

disadvantages of working together and which activities are best done individually or in teams.

Task 3 Evaluate a team activity

3.1 & 3.2 Small groups
Give the groups between ten and 15 minutes to come up with ideas and complete the table below. The groups should then be given a few minutes to prepare a brief presentation to be given to the class. Afterwards the groups should be given a few minutes to make a group decision about which idea was the most creative.

Exercise 3.2 encourages students to reflect on the creative discussion. As an extension, it might be useful to ask the groups to reflect on whether individuals' roles changed when their group had to evaluate other groups' performances.

This session could be concluded by asking the class what was the single most important thing they learnt about teamwork from the lesson.

Unit 3 – Effective team membership

At the end of this unit students will:
• be able to identify verbal and non-verbal clues during a conversation;
• have practised note-taking.

Task 1 Using verbal and non-verbal information

1.1 Individual work/pairwork/small group work
Answers:
1 (e); 2 (a); 3 (i); 4 (g); 5 (b); 6 (d); 7 (c); 8 (h); 9 (f).

1.2, 1.3 & 1.4 Small groups
These activities are student-led, so many answers are possible.

Task 2 Group observation

2.1 Group work
Ask students to work in groups of about five. Student A leads the discussion and makes notes in grid A. Student B does not take part in the discussion, but observes, making notes in grid B. All other students should close their books. The discussion should last no longer than 15 minutes.

2.2 Group work

Allow each group to spend up to ten minutes debriefing. The observers should feed back to the group, before the group as a whole addresses the discussion points listed. The main points made in each group could then be reported to the class and collected on the board in a final plenary session.

Unit 4 – Interactive dialogue

At the end of this unit students will have:

- discussed cultural differences and how to deal with them;
- considered the importance of maintaining balanced interaction in conversation.

Task 1 Cultural differences

1.1 Pairwork

Answers will vary from pair to pair. In a multicultural class it might be interesting to ask if the pair chose to compare their own two cultures or whether they compared their own cultures with one not belonging to either of the pair.

1.2 Pairwork

Ask students to work in pairs, deciding if the statements are true or false.

Answers:

a) T	e) T
b) F	f) T
c) F	g) F
d) T	

Ask students to reflect on the information given above. Elicit from them that the statements are about customs and traditions. Ask the students to name some traditions and customs from their own country. Then elicit if all the people in that country follow the same traditions and customs. Why/why not?

1.3 Small group work

Ask students to work in groups of four to six. Encourage them to make notes of their discussion. Ask students to share their ideas in a brief plenary session at the end of the activity.

Task 2 Talking at or talking to

2.1 Pairwork

Ask students to work in pairs on this exercise and give reasons for their opinions.
Possible answers might include:

a) B	d) A
b) A	e) B/A
c) B	

Answers to the questions in Exercise 2.2 are based on individual opinion.

Task 3 Team behaviour

3.1 Individual work

Answers:

A = vi
B = ii, iii, v
C = i, iv
D = vii

Students should compare their answers in groups, before moving on to Exercise 3.2.

3.2 Small group work

Ask students to feed back briefly to the whole class at the end of the activity.

Unit 5 – Encouraging interaction

At the end of this unit students will:

- be able to identify and use techniques for encouraging and discouraging interaction between people.

Task 1 Listening techniques

Strategy	Encourage	Discourage	It depends
Fidgeting		X	
Maintaining eye contact	X		
Scowling		X	
Smiling	X		
Head-nodding	X		
Looking down		X	
Making non-verbal noises such as 'uh-huh' or 'mm'	X		
Using exclamations such as: Really? Great! Wow!			X
Repeating key speaker words		X	
Asking questions	X		
Keeping silent			X
Folding your arms across your chest and sitting back in the chair		X	

1.1 Small group work
Follow the instructions in the course book.

Task 2 Deploying techniques

2.1, 2.2 & 2.3 Small group work
Allow about 20 minutes for each exercise. It is important that the group works through the debriefing questions after each discussion, possibly making notes of the more interesting points made so as to share them in a plenary session at the end of Task 2.

Task 3 Interaction issues

3.1 Pairwork/small group work
The answers to the questions will probably be affected by individual students' preferences, but possible answers include:
a) It might be useful to determine if the other person was shy, angry or was not maintaining eye contact for another reason. If the other speaker was shy, it would be worthwhile trying to build trust.
b) Refuse to have eye contact; say 'If I could just finish…'
c) Listen actively by nodding, maintaining eye contact, sitting in an attentive manner.
d) Do not assume that the person was bored as these forms of behaviour can have many meanings.
e) Praise the question and ask the questioner to answer his or her own question, e.g., 'That's an interesting question. What do you think?'

3.2 Plenary
Encourage students to focus on what they have learnt from the tasks in Unit 5.

Unit 6 – Ways of working with others

At the end of this unit students will:
• be more aware of the benefits of collaborating with a team;
• have discussed different teamwork activities.

Task 1 Examples of teamwork

1.1 & 1.2 Small group work
The students might need some help in seeing their own lives in terms of teamwork. Ask the students to work individually to complete the table first. Then ask them to share their ideas. After the students have completed Exercise 1.2, it might be useful to have a plenary session in which students report back about whether they had a big influence, or not, on the final decisions made. One possible extension would be to elicit examples of occasions when the students were not bothered that they had little influence and examples of occasions when their lack of influence was a problem for them.

Task 2 Studying in a team

2.1 & 2.2 Pairwork

Students should work individually to fill in the table and then compare ideas with a partner. Encourage students to explore the parameters within which, and the reasons why, their partners are happy, not happy or simply not bothered in the situations outlined.

2.3 & 2.4 Pairwork

Encourage students to give reasons for their answers. Conclude the session by choosing a couple of the statements that have inspired interest and eliciting views in a plenary.

Questions	Observer's comments
Did all the members of the group contribute or did some members dominate?	
What were the team's strengths and weaknesses?	
What techniques did they use to solve the problems?	
How well did the team keep to time?	
What was the team's score?	

Module 5

Problem-Solving

Unit 1 – What is problem-solving?

At the end of this unit students will have:
• become more aware of different types of problems and forms of problem-solving.

Task 1 Types of problems

One possible lead-in to the module and its aims might be to use the following quotation.
"Problems are only opportunities in work clothes."

You could either dictate the quotation to the class or copy it onto cards which the students rearrange to make the quotation. Then ask students to work in pairs to discuss the meaning of the quotation, whether they agree with it or not, and what support they can give for their opinion. Afterwards, focus the students on the introductory text and elicit the overall aim of Module 5.

1.1 Individual work

Elicit the problems shown in the visuals; then ask students to work individually, considering in which situations, both present and future, they face problems.

1.2 & 1.3 Small group work

These two exercises form a personalisation stage and so answers will vary. The tutor's role is to create an environment of trust. In a final plenary session, it might be useful to generalise the information collected in the groups, e.g., identify problems that tend to belong in your students' pasts, those that are predominant in their lives currently and those they feel might affect them in the future.

Task 2 Thinking about problem-solving

2.1 Pairwork

Ask the pairs of students to work through the five questions, making a note of the information that comes out of their discussions. These notes will be

used in a later lesson. This should take about ten minutes. Encourage students to share their ideas in a brief plenary.

2.2, 2.3 & 2.4 Pairwork

Ask the pairs of students to complete the table, column by column. In Exercise 2.4, encourage them to try and find at least two possible solutions.

Some possible answers might include:

Activity	Possible problem	Possible solution
1 Writing essays	understanding the task	• clarify with the tutor. • read essays by students in previous years.
2 Doing research	finding relevant information quickly	• practise using the blurb on the back of a book and the contents page to identify if a text is relevant. • use the rdn.ac.uk site to upgrade subject-specific search skills.
3 Giving presentations	going completely blank	• prepare keyword notes. • practise giving the presentation a couple of times.
Doing research projects		
Preparing case study evaluations		
Solving maths, physics or chemistry problems		
Sitting examinations		

It is impossible to predict students' answers, but problems often concern access to resources, time and data. Depending on the problems identified, possible solutions might be planning, time management, finding a good space to study, forming a study group, etc.

Task 3 Forms of problem-solving

Lead in by asking students to read the short introductory text and ask them which two categories of problem are mentioned in it: one-correct-solution problems and several-possible-answer problems. Then ask the students to put the problems depicted in the visuals into one of the categories.

3.1 Group work & 3.2 Plenary

Encourage your students to think about which of the problem types is/are most likely to be prevalent on their course. If they are not sure, they should be encouraged to consult student handbooks and past exam papers where possible.

Problem A requires an answer
Problem B requires the answerer to identify relevant material, analyse it and communicate its significance to the reader. There is no single answer possible.
Problem C requires the answerer to analyse the situation and the problem, to identify possible methodologies and criteria by which to judge them and, finally, to evaluate the potential success of the methodologies. There is no single answer.

3.3 Small group work

Encourage students to work through the problems, thinking about alternative solutions in groups of three (ABC).

3.4 Small group work

Now form three new groups: all As, all Bs and all Cs. Ask the groups to focus on whether there was a range of answers for each problem, or whether there was broad agreement on how to solve a particular problem. In a brief plenary session at the end of the task, elicit which problems tended to be solved in the same way by the class and which had a range of solutions.

Unit 2 – Problem-solving strategies

At the end of this unit students will be:
- more aware of how to evaluate different problems;
- more able to select appropriate strategies for dealing with them.

Task 1 Expectations in higher education

1.1 Individual work

Ask students to work through the exercise and compare answers with a partner.

Answers:

1 ability	5 resolution
2 features	6 success
3 strategies	7 critically
4 analyse	

1.2 Pairwork

Answers:

critically – explained by the text that follows the colon, i.e.:
'This means thinking critically to produce solutions: considering other viewpoints, looking for evidence and using experience when evaluating alternatives.'

analyse – an action that can be carried out on a problem and one that a student is expected to perform:
'You will be expected to analyse a problem ...'

strategy – strategies are mentioned several times, which suggests that they play an important role in problem-solving. They can be used to solve a given problem:
'Problem-solving in higher education settings refers to a student's ability to identify the main features of a given problem and to develop appropriate strategies for solving it.'

Task 2 Problems and solutions

One possible lead-in is to focus students' attention on the visual and elicit the problems depicted.

2.1 Pairwork

Refer the students back to Task 1 and point out that it gives a process for problem-solving. Ask them to follow this process in their discussions of the four problems:

a) analyse the problem by identifying its key features;

b) brainstorm different strategies for solving the problem;

c) identify criteria for evaluating the solutions and use them to do this.

Also point out to the students that there may be problems that have no solution and that what might appear to be a problem might, with the application of thinking, turn out not to be one.

2.2 Pairwork

Again refer the students back to Task 1 and the process for problem-solving.

2.3 & 2.4 Pairwork

Follow instructions in course book.

2.5 Pairwork

Encourage students to choose one problem to work through together.

2.6 Pairwork

Follow instructions in course book. Encourage students to make notes as they will be useful for the next exercise.

2.7 Group work

Divide the previous pairs into A students and B students. Ask two new groups to form: all the As and all the Bs. Ask the groups to find out the extent to which people's responses were similar.

Unit 3 – The problem-solving process

At the end of this unit students will:

• be more familiar with language used to describe problems and their solutions;

• have a better awareness of problem-solving procedures and techniques.

Task 1 The language used in problem-solving

1.1 Pairwork

Target verbs might include: analyse, brainstorm, choose, define, develop, discover, estimate, evaluate, find out, pose, prove, solve, weigh up

If your students struggle in the brainstorming stage, elicit the verbs, write them on the board and discuss similarities and differences in meaning.

1.2 Individual work/pairwork

Answers:

1 brainstorm
2 define
3 & 4 discuss/analyse/evaluate
5 choosing
6 weigh

Task 2 Steps to solving a problem

2.1 Pairwork

Answer:

d), e), a), c), b).

Task 3 A logical approach to problem-solving

3.1 & 3.2 Individual work/pairwork

Ask students to work individually and then compare their flow charts in pairs.

Answers:

Situation: Recent evidence confirms that global warming is melting the ice in Antarctica faster than had been previously thought.

Problem: Global economic and ecological impact of rising sea levels, especially in highly populated coastland areas of Asia; erosion of the coastline, flooding and reduction in drinking-water supplies.

Solutions: 1 local flood prevention measures; 2 education.

Evaluation: Solution 1 is only useful in the short term. Solution 2 is a long-term one. However, it can only help to minimise the impact, rather than prevent sea levels from rising.

3.3 Small group work

Ask students to read the chart and evaluate the solutions. Encourage students to think about how different solutions may be more or less effective in certain contexts. Also encourage the students to think about the criteria they use to evaluate the solutions. These two activities may help the groups to come up with further solutions.

End the activity with a quick plenary session. Collect the groups' various solutions on the board and ask the class to evaluate them.

3.4 Pairwork

Remind the students of the process that was set out in Task 1 of this unit. If an overhead projector or A1 paper are available, supply pairs with transparency/paper and pens and explain that they will give a mini-presentation on their work, talking the class through the pair's solutions and decision-making process in relation to choosing the best option. Tell the pairs they only have 30 minutes to work through the exercise and to prepare the visual aid and notes to speak from.

Unit 4 – Elaborating the problem

At the end of this unit students will:
* have become more familiar with solving case studies;
* have gathered information to find solutions to problems in an academic situation.

Task 1 Identifying problems

Ask students to discuss in pairs the meaning of the saying: *More haste, less speed.* Then ask them to read the introductory text and decide whether they were correct or not.

1.1 Small group work

Put students into groups of four. Direct their attention to the visuals and ask them to spend about ten minutes brainstorming problems they encountered when they first arrived at university.

1.2 Group work

Put the groups of four into pairs and ask them to see if they had the same problems, to discuss how they alleviated these problems and to give each other advice where appropriate.

Task 2 Defining the task

2.1 Pairwork

Ask students to look at the picture of Petra and guess how she is feeling. Then introduce the task, underlining that the students should spend time understanding her problem fully before finding solutions.

Possible answers:

What are Petra's problems?	• homesick • poor lecture-listening performance
Write the problem as questions + goals	• How can I alleviate my homesickness in order to function better? • How can I improve my listening performance in order to understand my lectures better? • Is there a link between the two problems and do I need to work on both of them?
Solutions	• find out about the support network at my university; • tell my personal tutor; • live with a host family or students who speak English fluently; • make English-speaking friends; • attend a study skills course; • take additional English lessons; • keep in regular contact with my family and friends.

Task 3 Gathering information

One possible lead-in is to ask students to speculate on the problem shown in the illustration. Then ask students to read through the problem, checking if their predictions were accurate.

3.1 Small group work

Possible answers:

What are the problems?	• time management re. essay and presentation • parents' arrival
Write the problem as questions + goals	• How can I improve my time management skills in order to submit my essay on time and give a good presentation? • How can I manage my time so that I can make my parents feel welcome?
Solutions	• ask my parents to visit in 12 days' time or suggest that they visit another city/relative in the UK before they visit me; • plan my time according to my new deadline (ten days' time not 12); • make an appointment with a tutor to discuss my essay plan and then write one before the appointment; • arrange for a friend to give me a hand by reading my first draft of the essay and giving me feedback; • start researching and writing the presentation after I've completed the first draft of the essay.

3.2 Pairwork/small group work

Give pairs of students ten minutes to create another problem and complete the grid. Ask two pairs of students to describe their imagined problems to each other. The pairs then work on their new problem for ten minutes. After this the groups of two pairs compare their work, explaining their reasoning.

3.3 Small group work

The groups of students now give their two problems to another group, which carries out the same process. If an overhead projector or A1 paper are available, supply groups with transparency/paper

and pens and explain that they will choose one of the problems and give a mini-presentation on their work, presenting their analysis of the problem and talking the class through the group's solutions.

Unit 5 – Finding the best solution

At the end of this unit students will be:
• more able to evaluate a solution objectively;
• more familiar with different problem-evaluation techniques.

Task 1 Deciding how to react

1.1 Small group work

Encourage students to justify their answer by giving precedents.

1.2 Individual work/pairwork

After students have worked through the exercise individually, ask them to compare their answers with a partner.

Answers:
1 range	6 expertise
2 ideas	7 objective
3 problems	8 matrix
4 drawbacks	9 conclusions
5 implemented	

Task 2 Paired comparison analysis

Individual work/pairwork

Ask students to work individually to discover which option from the grid the student chose. Ask them to compare their answer with their partner's.

It might be useful to have a plenary session at the end in which you compare answers to the exercise as a class and elicit other ideas from the students. Other ideas might include: encouraging others to speak; making sure people have time to think and answer; listening actively; respecting all opinions.

Task 3 Subjective versus objective evaluation

3.1 Individual work

Ask students to work individually, underlining examples of objective and subjective comments in the paragraphs.

3.2 Pairwork

Get students to compare their answers in pairs, justifying their opinions by referring to examples from the text.

Answers:

a) Text A = subjective: it uses personal forms, e.g., 'I', and is full of unsubstantiated claims, e.g., *English people speak the best form of English.*

Text B = objective: it uses impersonal forms, e.g., it structures and focuses on the criteria for making a decision about where to study rather than giving an unsubstantiated opinion, e.g., the size of tuition fees and the cost of living.

b) Text B appears to be more academic for the reasons given above.

Task 4 Writing a report

4.1 Individual work

This task could be set as homework. It would also lend itself to peer evaluation. Students could be asked to read through someone else's work and evaluate the writer's solution, making notes on a named post-it note that they stick to the essay. The essays could then form a wall display and students could be asked to select the best essay, in terms of the solution proposed and the best evaluative feedback.

Unit 6 – Creative thinking

At the end of this unit students will:
- be able to support and justify reasons for analysing alternatives and choosing options.

Task 1 Discussing solutions to problems

1.1 Individual work/pairwork

Ask students to work through the exercise individually and compare answers.

Answers:

1 e); 2 f); 3 b); 4 h); 5 a); 6 d); 7 c); 8 g).

Task 2 Putting techniques into practice

2.1, 2.2, 2.3, 2.4 & 2.5 Large group work

Follow the instructions in the course book. In a final plenary session, ask students to refer themselves back to the notes they made in Unit 1, Exercise 2.1 of the module and to reflect on the extent to which their thinking and problem-solving practice has developed. Ask them to think about:
- the most useful point they have learnt;
- the most surprising point they have learnt or change they have made in their thinking.

Critical Thinking

Unit 1 – What is critical thinking?

At the end of this unit students will:

- understand the difference between thinking and critical thinking;
- recognise the difference between a fact and an opinion;
- have a framework to evaluate arguments.

Task 1 Thinking skills

Explain to the class that the point of this exercise is not so much to get the right answer as to examine the process of finding a solution. As an alternative to Exercise 1.3, ask students to work with a partner and verbalise their thought process as they are doing the task.

1.1 Individual work
Answers:
- a) The ✗ should be circled.
- b) The ♥ should be circled.
- c) IL should be circled.
- d) ttf should be circled.

1.2 Individual work
Answers:
- a) ▲
- b) ✓
- c) 21 (8 + 13)
- d) 64 (32 x 2)

1.3 Pairwork
Your role here is to facilitate discussion.

Task 2 Critical thinking skills

2.1 Individual work
Depending on your students' level, you might need to pre-teach the following vocabulary:
a global language
to migrate
economic dominance
status

2.2 Pairwork
Answers:
- a) English has become a global language.
- b) Three reasons:
  - i) historical: the language migrated with native speakers to many parts of the world;
  - ii) easy to learn: simple grammar and vocabulary borrowed from many other languages;
  - iii) economic: economic dominance of some English-speaking countries.

- c) English is likely to remain the number-one global language for the foreseeable future.
- d) The three points do not support the conclusion as none of them explains the future dominance of English adequately.

Task 3 Facts or opinions?

Lead in by focusing your students' attention on the picture of the car and the two comments. Elicit which comment is an opinion and which is a fact.

3.1 Pairwork
English is a very easy language to learn. (opinion)
English is spoken all over the world. (fact)

3.2 Individual work/pairwork
a) English has borrowed many words from a wide range of other languages. Examples include 'tycoon' from Japanese, 'verandah' from Hindi, 'gong' from Javanese, 'slim' from Dutch and 'junta' from Spanish.

b) English is spoken in more countries than any other language.

c) English contains vocabulary which is borrowed from many other languages, and this is why it is a global language.

3.3 Pairwork
Some suggested answers:
a) Decisions about the practice of cloning should be made by experts who understand the science involved, not by the general public. Discuss.

- Decisions about the practice of cloning need to be made on a scientific basis (not on another one, e.g., ethical).
  - The general public does not understand the science involved in cloning.

b) Outline the main measures for the prevention of cancer.
  - Cancer can be prevented.
  - There is more than one way of preventing cancer.

c) A knowledge of Economics is essential for historians. Discuss.
  - Historians need to know about Economics.

d) One of the causes of juvenile delinquency is a result of poor attachment from birth. What might other causes be?
  - Poor attachment at birth leads to juvenile delinquency.
  - Other causes lead to juvenile delinquency.

Task 4 Questioning opinions

Small group work
Some suggested answers:

a) What is the practice of cloning? Are decisions about the practice of cloning necessary? If so, what needs to be decided about the practice of cloning? What criteria should we use to decide who should make the decisions? Would this group accept the decision-making role?

b) What is cancer? What causes cancer? Can cancer be prevented? If so, how can it be prevented?

c) Why do historians need to know about Economics? How much and what kind of knowledge do they need?

d) What is juvenile delinquency? What is attachment? What is poor attachment? What causes poor attachment? Does poor attachment lead to juvenile delinquency? Do other factors lead to juvenile delinquency?

Task 5 A check list for evaluating research

Individual work
Answers:
  a) unbiased
  b) research
  c) concepts
  d) reasoning
  e) viewpoints

Task 6 Putting evaluation into practice

6.1 Pairwork
The artificial language Esperanto would be a more appropriate global language than English in the twenty-first century. Discuss.

6.2 Pairwork
Some suggested answers:
  - What is an artificial language?
  - What is Esperanto and how did it develop?
  - Why was Esperanto developed?
  - What is a global language?
  - Is Esperanto a global language?
  - Is English a global language?
  - Will a global language exist in the 21st century?
  - If so, what will the needs of a global language be in the twenty-first century?
  - What criteria could we use to decide what makes a language appropriate as a global language?
  - Would one language be appropriate for everyone?
  - If not, for whom would Esperanto be appropriate and for whom would it not be appropriate?
  - For whom would English be appropriate and for whom would it not be appropriate?

6.3 Individual work/pairwork
Depending on the needs of your class, the following vocabulary might need to be pre-taught:
- to address something to someone
- to base something on something
- estimates vary widely
- something is evidence of something
- given that…
- to invent something
- to overtake something
- to reject (a proposal)
- to sign a petition in favour of something
- to date (i.e., until now)
- to set out to do something
- a universal language

6.4 Individual work/pairwork
This task could be set for homework and discussed in class at a later date or handed in to you.

Unit 2 – Recognising strong or sound arguments

At the end of this unit students will be able to:
- identify parts of arguments;
- understand the relationship between parts of an argument.

Task 1 Constructing an argument

1.1 Pairwork
Global warming is definitely happening. I don't care what people say, but it was hotter this year than it has ever been.

1.2 Pairwork
Answers:
   a) Ali doesn't have a visa.
   b) Natalia is travelling by train.

1.3 Pairwork
Answers:
   a) Sarah Rollings will win the next election.
   b) My cousin will experience a loss in profits.

Task 2 Recognising sound or strong arguments

2.1 Individual work/pairwork
Answers:
   a) Some manufactured food products contain nuts. Harry is severely allergic to nuts therefore he should avoid certain manufactured foods.
   b) My aunt has sent me a cheque every year since I was five years old. Therefore I expect to receive a cheque for my birthday this year too.
   c) All Chinese people are good cooks. Ting Ting is Chinese so, as a consequence, she must be a good cook.

2.2 Individual work/pairwork
Answers:
   a) sound
   b) strong
   c) valid

Task 3 Checking your understanding

3.1 Pairwork
Answers:
   a) false
   b) false
   c) true

3.2 Pairwork
Answers:
   a) ii)(The food in this restaurant is <u>always</u> good = general; today = particular)
   b) i) (All dogs are black = not true.)
   c) iii)

3.3 Individual work/pairwork
Answers:
   a) strong   d) sound
   b) valid   e) sound
   c) valid   f) strong

Task 4 Your examples

4.1, 4.2 & 4.3 Individual work
These exercises could be set as homework.

4.4 Pairwork
You could use your students' work in this exercise to make a wall display.

Unit 3 – Recognising poor arguments

At the end of this unit students will be able to:
- recognise weak arguments;
- point out weak arguments politely.

Task 1 Spotting fallacious arguments

1.1 Individual work
Answers:

<u>Pita speaks Spanish</u> so <u>he must have come from Spain originally.</u>

1.2 Individual work/pairwork
Answers:
a) <u>He hasn't replied</u> so <u>he can't have received my letter.</u>
   There may be other reasons, e.g., he chose not to reply.
b) <u>He does not wear glasses</u> so <u>he must have excellent eyesight.</u>
   Maybe he is wearing contact lenses. Maybe he doesn't like glasses.
c) <u>English is superior to other languages</u> and, as a result, <u>it is a global language.</u>
   There may be a number of explanations why a language gains global status, e.g., economic power, colonisation.

Task 2 Poor argumentation strategies

2.1 Individual work
Answers:
a) being subjective = 3
b) appealing to common beliefs = 4
c) invoking peer pressure = 1
d) attempting to make others annoyed = 2

2.2 Individual work/pairwork
Answers:
a) = d) attempting to make others annoyed
b) = b) appealing to common beliefs
c) = a) being subjective
d) = c) invoking peer pressure

Task 3 Checking your understanding

3.1 Individual work/pairwork
Answers:
1 c) invoking peer pressure
2 a) being subjective
3 d) attempting to make others angry
4 b) appealing to common beliefs

3.2 Individual work/pairwork
Model a few examples for your students, before setting them to work on the exercise.
Possible answers include:
1 That's a bit over the top, isn't it?
2 Yes, but that is not a hundred per cent true in all cases, is it? Don't you think that in some cases …?
3 I know what you mean, but that seems a little extreme as a view.
4 Yes, that's one point of view, but wouldn't you agree that …?

Unit 4 – Persuasion through language or pressure

At the end of this unit students will be able to:
- recognise when language, rather than reason, is used to persuade;
- recognise when pressure, rather than reason, is used to persuade.

Lead in by asking students to read the introductory text and answer the question: *What does the text compare arguing with?*

Task 1 Making an idea sound better or worse

1.1 Small group work
One possible lead-in would be to focus students' attention on the visual and ask whether they see a freedom fighter or a terrorist. Then ask them to read the text and find out which term, *terrorist* or *freedom fighter*, is a euphemism.

Ask your students to discuss the questions in small groups. You could round up with a brief plenary.

1.2 Individual work/pairwork

One lead-in might be to bring a picture of a famous, slim model/film star to class and elicit if he/she is too thin or not. Alternatively, ask your students what they know about the size-zero issue.

Answers:
Euphemisms: slim, willow-like, svelte, fine-boned
/juːfɪmɪzəmz/
Dysphemisms: skinny, bony, skeletal, scrawny
/dɪsfɪmɪzəmz/

1.3 Pairwork
Possible answers:
- body language and context at the time
- a good dictionary after the event

1.4 Pairwork
Possible answers include:
(i) **euphemisms**: bathroom, W.C., powder-room; **dysphemisms**: bog
(ii) **euphemisms**: to remove, to take out, to put out of its misery; **dysphemisms**: to slaughter
(iii) **euphemisms**: have a fuller figure; **dysphemisms**: lardy

Task 2 Making something sound less important or serious

Lead in by asking students to look at the cartoon and explain the joke. Elicit if this answer would be common in their culture.

2.1 Individual work/pairwork
Answers:
a) He is just a teacher.
b) It costs a mere £20 a month to insure your life.
c) She got her 'degree' from a university in the Midlands (or She got her degree from a 'university' in the Midlands).

2.2 Pairwork
Answers:
a) A teacher is really unimportant.
b) £20 is a small amount of money to pay in order to insure your life.
c) Her qualification is not up to the standard of a degree/Her institution is not up to the standard of a university.

Task 3 Making something seem more important or serious

Lead in by asking the class to name the singer in the photo. Then ask if they consider Mick Jagger to be the most inventive singer who ever lived. Explain that some might say that this claim is an over-statement or hyperbole. /haɪpɜːbəlɪ/

One possible lead-in would be to ask your students to speculate what the problem is in each of the three photos.
Possible answers:
a) headache ≠ serious illness (possibly used in order to get time off work)
b) fascists ≠ parents who ask their children to be home by midnight (possibly used to get sympathy from the listener)
c) extreme superlative (possibly used to dissuade the listener from going to see it)

3.2 Individual/small group work
End this activity with a brief plenary in which groups share their favourite hyperbole with the rest of the class.

Task 4 Pressuring the audience

4.1 Individual work/pairwork
'Anyone with half a brain understands that a natural language is better than an artificial one.' (b)

'It is clearly the case that Esperanto is easier to learn than English.' (a)

'Any educated person understands the value of English.' (b)

'Anyone can see that Esperanto could be learnt in weeks.' (a)

'As is universally acknowledged, English will always be the best global language.' (a)

'All intelligent people naturally recognise Esperanto's superiority over English.' (b)

Task 5 Checking your understanding

5.1 Individual work
Ask students to underline any words and phrases

the two speakers use to try and influence each other unfairly.

Answers:
  A: <u>Anyone with half a brain</u> can see that Esperanto is an easier language to learn than English. It doesn't have any irregular verbs...and it has <u>the smallest vocabulary ever of any language</u>.
  B: But the <u>'language'</u> [the speaker makes a gesture with both hands] of Esperanto is <u>totally unknown</u>. Who speaks it? <u>No one.</u>
  A: Unknown! It has <u>one or two fewer speakers than English</u>, but <u>the difference in numbers is minimal</u>.
  B: <u>You're joking!</u> Esperanto has <u>a handful of speakers</u> and there's a reason for that. It's OK for <u>chit-chat</u>, but you can't have a serious conversation in it.
  A: <u>Well we're speaking English now and I wouldn't call this a serious conversation!</u>

5.2 Pairwork
Get pairs to check through their work together, possibly categorising the different abuses of language and pressure tactics.

Unit 5 – Detecting bias

At the end of this unit students will be able to:
- consider sources of bias in evidence in academic research;
- identify possible reasons for researcher bias.

Task 1 Detecting possible bias – Interviews

1.1 Small group work
Possible reasons include:
  The interviewee wants to present himself/herself in the best light.
  The interviewee is influenced by the role/identity of the interviewee.
  The interviewee might not feel free to speak honestly for political reasons.

1.2 Small group work
Possible answers include:
  a) The interviewer might affect the interaction due to his/her experience of interviewing, gender, language choices, clothing style, decision to

share personal experiences with the interviewee, the ratio of interviewers to interviewees, eye contact, etc.
  b) He/she can minimise her/his impact by introducing herself/himself clearly but briefly, using non-sexist and non-racist language, dressing in a neutral way for the context, not sharing personal experiences, not outnumbering interviewees, using eyecontact in a neutral way for the context, etc.

Task 2 Detecting possible bias – Researchers and sources of funding

2.1 Small group work
Answers:
  a) The researcher might feel pressure to find positive outcomes for his/her sponsors.
  b) The library staff might feel pressure to find positive outcomes in terms of saving their jobs.
  c) The British researcher might be biased against or for the group of migrants, depending on his/her prior experience.
  d) The researcher might feel pressure to find positive outcomes for his/her sponsors.
  e) The course director might emphasise the positive outcomes and minimise the negative outcomes.

Task 3 Avoiding bias

3.1 Individual work
Ask students to note down next to each element their own personal data. Then ask them which elements might be relevant.

Probable answers:
  a), b), d), e), g), h), I), k), l).

3.2 Pairwork/individual work
Encourage students to add any further elements that might be added. Get them to link their ideas with a particular piece of writing, e.g., *If I were writing a report on the dangers of cigarette smoking, I might mention that I am strongly anti-smoking.*

3.3 Individual work
This activity could be set for homework.

Unit 6 – Putting it into practice

At the end of this unit students will be able to:
- use critical thinking skills to construct arguments;
- evaluate their own and others' arguments;
- recognise different styles of arguing;
- put together the skills they have developed in the earlier parts of the module.

Task 1 Understanding the question

Lead in by asking students to explain what they see in the visual. Then ask them to underline the key words in the discussion question. Elicit the link between the visual and the question.

1.1 & 1.2 Small group work/pairwork

Your role here is to monitor the discussion. It might be useful to ask the groups to feed back on any interesting points in a brief plenary session at the end of the activities.

1.3 Individual work

This exercise lends itself to a quick revision of the principles and process of paraphrasing. Elicit these from the students.

Answers you could expect include:

Principles: restatement of the original; do not omit any ideas; do not add any ideas, including the opinion of the paraphraser; likely to need more words than the original; ideas should be expressed clearly for intended audience.

Process: understand the key words; understand the claim; make notes, using symbols and abbreviations where possible and changing the original text's vocabulary where necessary; organise the ideas into a sequence that fits the needs of the paraphraser's text and writing the paraphrase.

Depending on the needs of your students, this task could be extended to include peer evaluation as well as teacher evaluation and language feedback. To aid peer evaluation, it might be useful to provide a set of points for students to work through, e.g.:
- Does the paraphrase alter the meaning of the original?
- Does the paraphrase add meaning to the original?
- Is the paraphrase clearly expressed?

Task 2 Your view

2.1 Individual work

If necessary, model the exercise for your class by extemporising your thoughts as you decide where to place your cross on the first continuum. Alternatively, invite a student to do this.

2.2 Pairwork

This exercise provides an opportunity to practise giving reasons in speech.

2.3 Small group work

This exercise provides an opportunity to practise hypothesising and mitigating in speech.

Task 3 Gathering information

3.1 Small group work

If students get stuck, encourage them to look back at the keywords they underlined at the start of Unit 6 and get them to brainstorm questions: *How? Who? Where? When? What? How many? How often?*, etc.

3.2 Individual work

This exercise could either be set for homework or could form a library-based lesson. Encourage students to make a note of all the relevant bibliographical information for any sources they take notes from. It might be useful to revise what information this is for the different kinds of source, e.g., book, journal, website.

For more information, see *TASK* Module 10: *Research and Referencing*.

3.3 Small group work

You could ask students to submit their evaluation of an argument they have found to you, using the criteria in Unit 1, Task 5 of this module as a framework.

You could also ask students to look out for examples of writers persuading their audience through language or pressure and examples of where researchers' outcomes have been biased by sources of income, etc. These examples could be collected as a wall display or entered into a project blog.

Task 4 Developing your argument(s)

4.1, 4.2 & 4.3 Individual work
These exercises could be set as homework.

4.4 Pairwork
It might be helpful to revise some forms of indirect/mitigated language for the feedback session. Native English-speaking tutors often use this type of language in their spoken feedback to students and do not realise that it is often difficult for non-native speakers to interpret.

Introduce the activity by giving examples of this type of language and asking students what the sentences actually mean, e.g.:

'I like the point you made about preserving traditional cultures, but it was perhaps overstated.' (*Your evidence doesn't match the strength of your opinion*.)

'Your conclusion came as something of a surprise.' (Either: *You concluded suddenly without fully developing your argument*; or: *This piece of work is too short*; or: *Your conclusion does not match the rest of your argument.*)

Task 5 Developing counter-arguments

5.1 Individual work
Model this activity for the class and then elicit some further examples of arguments and counter-arguments.

5.2 Pairwork
Encourage students to make notes as these will come in handy during the seminar.

Task 6 The seminar
If you have a large group, or a mixture of quiet and talkative students, you might want to consider a 'daisy seminar'. Sit half the students in an inward-facing circle. Each of the remaining students chooses an already-seated partner and sits behind him/her, facing outwards. The inner-circle students participate in the seminar, while the outer-circle students remain silent and make notes on their partners' arguments. When the first group has completed the seminar the students swap places with their partners and the activity is repeated. These notes then provide a good record for Task 7.

Task 7 Evaluating the arguments
As an extension to this task, you could ask students to work in small groups to write a short bibliography containing the six most useful sources on the topic. This would involve them in using their research notes and evaluation skills and could be tied in with *TASK* Module 10: *Research and Referencing*

Introduction to IT Skills

Introduction

IT skills audit

It is possible that within your group there may be a wide variation in the level of students' IT skills. In order to use this module most effectively, it may be worthwhile carrying out an IT skills audit. The results of this could then be used to identify areas unknown to most of the group. In a situation where some students feel confident of their skills and others less so, it may be possible to set particular units for self-study or to pair proficient students with less proficient students.

On page 51 there is a photocopiable IT skills questionnaire. The form below can be used to make a note of the results of the survey.

Using *Word*		1	2	3	4	5
1	Opening a document					
2	Using the spell checker					
3	Using the grammar checker					
4	Adding a header or a footer to a page					
5	Inserting a table					
6	Changing the line spacing on a document					
7	Changing the margins on a document					
8	Using different toolbars, e.g., drawing, formatting, tables, borders					
9	Changing the font style					
10	Adding bullet points					
11	Centring text					
12	Putting text in bold					
13	Putting text in italics					
14	Moving around a document quickly					
15	Moving text within a document					
16	Adding page numbers					
17	Adding footnotes					
18	Indenting text					
19	Sending a document as an e-mail attachment					
20	Storing documents in different drives					
21	Creating different folders in which to save documents					
Using spreadsheets		1	2	3	4	5
22	Creating a spreadsheet					
23	Using formulae to do calculations					
24	Using functions to do calculations					
Using *Excel* to produce charts and graphs		1	2	3	4	5
25	Selecting the best visual form for your data					
26	Creating graphs					
27	Making your graph as clear as possible					

IT Skills Questionnaire

The following questionnaire is designed to find out in which areas of IT you are confident and in which areas you are less knowledgeable. This information will help your tutor to plan your classes.

Fill in the following questionnaire.

1= need to improve this skill considerably; 5 = excellent – no need to improve this skill

Using *Word*						
1	Opening a document	1	2	3	4	5
2	Using the spell checker	1	2	3	4	5
3	Using the grammar checker	1	2	3	4	5
4	Adding a header or a footer to a page	1	2	3	4	5
5	Inserting a table	1	2	3	4	5
6	Changing the line spacing on a document	1	2	3	4	5
7	Changing the margins on a document	1	2	3	4	5
8	Using different toolbars, e.g., drawing, formatting, tables, borders	1	2	3	4	5
9	Changing the font style	1	2	3	4	5
10	Adding bullet points	1	2	3	4	5
11	Centring text	1	2	3	4	5
12	Putting text in bold	1	2	3	4	5
13	Putting text in italics	1	2	3	4	5
14	Moving around a document quickly	1	2	3	4	5
15	Moving text within a document	1	2	3	4	5
16	Adding page numbers	1	2	3	4	5
17	Adding footnotes	1	2	3	4	5
18	Indenting text	1	2	3	4	5
19	Sending a document as an e-mail attachment	1	2	3	4	5
20	Storing documents in different drives	1	2	3	4	5
21	Creating different folders in which to save documents	1	2	3	4	5
Using spreadsheets						
22	Creating a spreadsheet	1	2	3	4	5
23	Using formulae to do calculations	1	2	3	4	5
24	Using functions to do calculations	1	2	3	4	5
Using *Excel* to produce charts and graphs						
25	Selecting the best visual form for your data	1	2	3	4	5
26	Creating graphs	1	2	3	4	5
27	Making your graph as clear as possible	1	2	3	4	5

Unit 1 – Creating a document

At the end of this unit students should:
- know more about choices they can make when creating a document by studying the menu options;
- be able to use the toolbar effectively.

The answers given below for this module assume that you and your students are using *Word* 2003 for PCs. As is often the case, you may find some variation to the answers given as IT software allows many possible options. The answers are thus a guide rather than definitive.

Task 1 Getting ready

If you have carried out an IT skills audit, you might want to get the students to collate the results. This would allow the group to get a sense of their collective needs and also of their individual strengths and weaknesses. Moreover, if you intend to pair weaker and stronger students, it gives you and/or your students useful information upon which to base a pairing decision. You could also use this information to prepare a spreadsheet and then a visual aid (Units 5 & 6).

1.1 Individual work/pairwork
As suggested in the course book.

Task 2 Menu options

2.1 Individual work/pairwork
You may need to check/pre-teach the following vocabulary:
to format a document;
a hyperlink;
a header/footer;
utilities.

It might also be worthwhile eliciting which of the technical words listed (e.g., *tools*, *table*, *window*) have a different meaning in everyday English.

Answers:
- a) Tools>Spelling & Grammar
- b) Format>Paragraph
- c) Insert>Hyperlink
- d) Help>Microsoft Word Help
- e) Table>Insert>Table
- f) View>Header and footer

2.2 Pairwork
Ask students to compare their answers.

2.3 Individual work
Ask students to minimise *Word* by clicking the icon in the top right-hand corner of the screen before they do this exercise. When they have finished, ask them to check their work by clicking on the different menus.

2.4 Small group work
- a) Answers will vary according to individual students' experience.
- b) In order to prepare students for Unit 3, it might be worth asking them if they have looked at the student handbook for their future university course. These handbooks are often available online. It might be useful for your students to use these to find out about their future university department's preferred layout and presentation of written coursework.

Task 3 Using the *Help* menu

3.1 Individual work/pairwork
Ask students to work through questions a) and b). When they have answered these, get pairs of students to work together. Ask them to compare the benefits of using Microsoft *Word* **Help** and **Office Assistant** to find out more about the spell and grammar checkers. Which method do they prefer and why?

Answers:
- a) As suggested in the course book.
- b) Microsoft *Word* **Help**; show the **Office Assistant**.
- c) According to individual preference.

Task 4 Learn more about menu options

4.1 & 4.2 Individual work/pairwork

	What the menu option is for	Key commands
e	choose a name for your document	
k	print a document	Ctrl + P
c	close the active document without exiting *Word* completely	
d	save a document for later use	Ctrl + S
m	find out who wrote the original document and other details	
f	save a document for viewing on web browser	
a	create a new document	Ctrl + N
i	change the margins and layout of your page	
j	see what the printed version of your page will look like	
h	preview a web page	
o	close down *Word* after prompting you to save	
l	send your document to someone by e-mail	
b	open an existing document	Ctrl + O
g	find earlier versions of the same document	

4.3 Pairwork/small group work

Ask students to divide up the menus in their pair/group. Each student should then select a number of options and utilities from his/her menus and prepare notes to give a spoken description of their purposes. You might need to model this for the class before your students start making notes.

For example, *this gives you statistics about a piece of text or a document – the number of pages, words, characters, paragraphs and lines in the text or document. What is it?* (Answer = Tools>Word Count).

When the students have finished preparing their notes, encourage them to quiz each other.

4.4 & 4.5 Individual work/pairwork

Alternatively, Exercise 4.4 could be set as homework and you could start the next class with Exercise 4.5.

Task 5 Practical work

It might be useful to conclude the class by collecting your students' answers to Exercise 5.3 on the board and then asking them to look through the course book to find out which units correspond to the needs they have identified.

Unit 2 – Modifying and manipulating text

At the end of this unit students will:
- understand more about the choices they can make when creating a document;
- be able to highlight, modify and move text around.

Task 1 Familiarise yourself with toolbars and icons

1.1 Individual work/pairwork
Answers:
    a) probably 18, though this may vary if the computer has added software with toolbars available
    b) This may vary.

1.2 Individual work/pairwork
You might need to check/pre-teach the following vocabulary:
    mouse;
    cursor;
    table;
    border.

Answers:
    a) under the menu option
    b) under the menu option
    c) bottom of the page
    d) under the menu option

1.3 Individual work/pairwork

You may need to check/pre-teach the following vocabulary:

image;

visual impact;

to enhance (something);

to give (alternative) access to (something);

basic utilities;

font;

set of tools.

Answers:

i) c   iii) d

ii) a   iv) b

Task 2 Explore ways of using icons

2.1 Pairwork

Answers:

a)   e)

b)   f)

c)   g)

d)   h)

Task 3 Navigating a document

3.1 & 3.2 Individual work/pairwork

Function	Scrollbar	Key
Scroll up the document	Single up arrow/drag side rectangle upwards	↑ direction key
Scroll down the document	Single down arrow/drag side rectangle downwards	↓ direction key
Scroll to the left	Single left arrow/drag bottom rectangle to left	← direction key
Scroll to right	Single right arrow/drag bottom rectangle to right	→ direction key
Jump from left to right		Tab key
Jump up the document by one page	Double up arrow	Page Up key
Jump down the document by one page	Double down arrow	Page Down key

If your students are already familiar with these options, ask them to click on the small circle between the double up and double down arrows on the scroll bar. Elicit what additional ways there are of navigating a document.

Your students might also like to know that **Ctrl + Home** takes them to the start of a document and **Ctrl + End** takes them to the end of a document.

Task 4 Highlighting and moving text

4.1 & 4.2 Individual work

Students follow the instructions in their course books.

4.3 Group work

Answers:

a) copies highlighted text

b) cuts highlighted text

c) pastes highlighted text

Tasks 5 & 6 Using the horizontal ruler/Using what you have learnt

Students follow the instructions in their course books.

Unit 3 – Word-processing academic documents

At the end of this unit students will:
- be more familiar with academic conventions;
- be able to use headers and footers effectively;
- be more confident about using the spell and grammar check to edit their work.

Task 1 Understanding house style

1.1 Pairwork
One lead-in would be to ask students to search the Internet for departmental student handbooks related to a subject they wish to study, as many of these are now available online.

Possible answers include:
- a) • to have a standardised format
     • to make sure the author is anonymous – often students are asked to put their candidate number on their work, but not their name, so that marking is as unbiased as possible
     • to practise following (professional/academic) rules
     • to show that students belong to a particular academic community

  b) Answers depend on the students' educational institutions, past and present.

1.2 Individual work/pairwork/plenary
You might need to check/pre-teach the following:
double/single/one-and-a-half (line) spacing;
margin;
justified text;
pagination/page number;
indented text;
quotations;
footnotes/endnotes.

It might be necessary to check the answers to this in a plenary session.

1.3 Pairwork
a) Format>Paragraph>Line spacing <u>or</u> highlight the text and then Ctrl+2/Ctrl+1/Ctrl+5
b) File>Page Set Up>Margins
c) ▤
d) View>Header and Footer
e) Insert>Page Numbers
f) Highlight text and click on ruler
g) Highlight text and click on font choices or size choices ▲ Normal ▾ Tahoma ▾ 10 ▾
h) Insert>Footnotes>Footnotes

Task 2 Formatting an academic assignment

2.1 & 2.2 Individual work/pairwork
Students' work should look like this:

OVERSEAS STUDENTS

IN THE UK

Introduction

Ask students to compare their work with the wrong answer given in the course book. Elicit the mistakes in the wrong answer.

Answers:
- wrong font
- title isn't centred
- title isn't all uppercase
- 'Introduction' heading is missing

Task 3 Setting headers and footers

Tasks 3.1 & 3.2 Individual work/pairwork
To insert a footer: **View>Header and Footer>Click on** ▤ **>**enter your information and use the formatting toolbar to choose your point size and add bold.

Task 4 Using the spell and grammar check

4.1 Individual work/pairwork
Answers:
- a) Press the ✓ icon on the Standard Toolbar <u>or</u> **Tools>Spelling and Grammar**.
- b) Highlight the piece of text to be checked and then do either option given in a).

4.2 Individual work/pairwork

Answers may vary to the first part of the task, but useful information could include:

- misspellings that do not exist in English
- lack of subject–verb agreement
- grammar forms that do not exist, e.g., two possessive pronouns in a row.

If students find the second part of the task difficult, point them to the next exercise.

4.3 Individual work/pairwork

Answers:

a) The more documents you create, the more untidy your 'My documents' page will look. **(Two possessive pronouns in a row.)**

b) A database consists of information which has been ordered and presented in a particular way. **(The checker tends to remind the writer that '*which*' or '*that*' might be possible, but does not tell the writer if a defining or non-defining relative clause is required.)**

c) Quickly carry out the following operations. **(The checker may confuse the adverb '*quickly*' with a noun as the subject of the sentence. As a result, it may offer '*carries*' as a suitable subject–verb agreement form.)**

d) You should write a short user guide that could be used by another student. **(The checker tends to select all passive verbs as potentially wrong and offers the writer the choice of using an active form.)**

As a final classroom or homework task, you might want to give your students a house style description for your institution and a document with a number of formatting, spelling and grammar errors in it and ask them to correct all the errors they can find.

Unit **4** – Filing and sending documents

At the end of this unit students will:

- be more confident about how to store documents in files on different drives;

- be able to send attachments by e-mail.

Task 1 Filing documents

As a lead-in, focus students on the visual and elicit what problems the writer may have in finding documents.

1.1 & 1.2 Pairwork

Students follow the instructions in their course books.

1.3 Small group work

Answers:

a) Click on the file, hold the cursor down and drag the file on top of the folder.

b) Click the *Modern Philosophy* folder, hold the cursor down and drag the folder on top of the *Philosphy* folder.

c) • **View>Arrange icons by>Name.**
   • **View>List.**
   • **View>Details.**

Task 2 Saving to a folder

2.1 Pairwork

If your students find this point difficult to explain, direct them to Exercise 2.2.

2.2 Individual work/pairwork

Answers:

a) Click on the File menu options.

b) Click Save within the *File* menu.

c) If the name of the folder next to *Save* in is not correct, click on the arrow next to the folder name. Then click the correct folder.

d) Type the name of document you wish to save.

e) Click Save.

Task 3 Using a memory stick

3.1 Pairwork

Answers could include:
   e-mail as an attachment
   burn onto a CD

3.2 Individual work/pairwork

Possible answers include:

Method	Advantages	Disadvantages
memory stick	quick to transfer data; the most durable form of portable storage; can store relatively large documents	can't store as much data as a CD; may not be affordable for students
e-mail	quick to send	both computers must be connected to the Internet; large attachments can be slow to send; some email programs block large attachments
burn onto CD	quick to download the data; can transfer a large amount of data	not all computers have CD burners; CDs can be scratched/damaged without proper care

3.3 & 3.4 Individual work

Students follow the instructions in their course books.

Task 4 Sending attachments

4.1 Individual work/pairwork

Students follow the instructions in their course books.

4.2 Individual work/pairwork

Answers:

Right-click on the document you wish to send.
Select Send to.
Then left-click on Mail Recipient.
Type the e-mail address of the recipient.
Type the subject if you wish.
Write a message to the recipient if you wish.
Left-click on Send.

4.3 Individual work/pairwork

Students follow the instructions in their course books.

4.4 Individual work/large group work

Students follow the instructions in their course books.

4.5 Pairwork/small group work

One possible activity is to integrate the course book task with some listening practice. Choose two songs, prepare a copy of each song's lyrics and have a playable version of each song.

Divide students into AB pairs (or AABB pairs). Give A students the lyrics for one song and B students the lyrics for the other song. Ask both A and B students to type the lyrics in a new document, if you haven't provided them with an electronic copy, and to make changes to the lyrics, for example substituting rhyming words (eye/pie) or changing spellings of homophones (break/brake). When A and B have finished, they should save their work in an appropriate folder and e-mail the 'new' lyrics to their partner using one of the methods from Exercises 4.2 and 4.3. A and B should now find all the errors they can and mark them in the text. They could use **Tools>Track changes** to do this. They should then e-mail their work back to their partner, who accepts all the correct changes and types the number of outstanding errors. A and B should e-mail their document back to their partner. Then play both songs so that students can check their work, add their final corrections and send the document back to their partner for a final check.

Unit 5 – Understanding and using spreadsheets

At the end of this unit the students will:

- understand the benefits of using spreadsheets rather than word-processing programs for some operations;
- be familiar with how to tabulate numerical information and apply formulae to tables.

Task 1 What spreadsheets are for

As a lead-in, focus students on the visuals and elicit possible uses of spreadsheets.

1.1 Small group work

Students follow the instructions in their course books.

Task 2 Using *Excel*

2.1 Pairwork
Answers are circled.

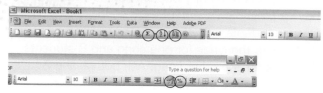

2.2 Pairwork
Data

2.3 Pairwork
Possible answers:

Menu option	Features that do not appear in Microsoft Word	Functions
File	Print area	Allows you to choose parts of the spreadsheet that you want to print
File	Save workspace	Allows more than one person to work together on a document and save changes to it
Edit	Delete sheet	Allows you to delete one or more sheets of data
View	Page break preview	Allows you to see how data on a large sheet will be divided up on different pages when it is printed

Task 3 Creating cells

3.1 & 3.2 Individual work
Students follow course book instructions.

3.3 Pairwork
Students can take it in turns to elicit information from each other, e.g.:
D3? – Bangles Ltd's income from Spain
B5? – Davis Ltd's income from France

Task 4 Using formulae

4.1 Individual work/pairwork
This formula is correct.

Task 5 Creating your own formulae

5.1 Individual work
Answer:
=(B2+C2+D2)/3

Note: The brackets are necessary, otherwise D2 is divided by 3 and the result added to B2 and C2.

5.2 Individual work
If students have done this correctly, they will get the following totals.
Apollo Ltd   1,670,167
Bangles Ltd   3,916,667
Corgi Ltd   3,966,833
Davis Ltd   4,697,333

Task 6 Using functions

6.1 Pairwork
Answer:
=SUM(B2:D2)

6.2 Individual work
a) This is the formula students need to use.
=SUM(B2:B5)
b) If students have done this correctly, they will get the following results.
France   8,800,500
Germany   6,430,000
Spain   5,081,500

Task 7 Exploring functions
Students follow course book instructions.

Unit 6 – Creating charts and graphs

At the end of this unit students will:
- feel more confident about choosing the appropriate chart or graph to represent their data;
- understand how to create a chart or graph using Excel.

Task 1 Choosing the right chart

1.1 Individual work
Answers:

Left to right: pie chart; column (or bar) chart; line graph

1.2 Pairwork

a) pie chart
b) line graph
c) column chart

1.3 Pairwork
Answer given in Task 2: 'Probably the most effective method of displaying the data collected in the European export database is by bar chart. This enables the viewer to compare each company's income gained from different countries.'

Tasks 2 & 3 Creating/refining your chart

Students follow instructions in course book.

Task 4 Explore other types of charts and graphs

4.1 Small group work/plenary
In groups of four to five, students each try out a different format for presenting the European export data. Encourage them to make notes and ask them to report back to the rest of the class in a plenary session.

4.2 Pairwork

Chart type	Useful for ...
Pie chart	showing proportions of a whole
Column/bar chart	comparing differences between categories
Line graph	• showing continuous data • showing how one thing is affected by another
Doughnut	showing proportions of a whole
Scatter	showing the relationship between numerical variables

Essay Writing

Unit 1 – Getting organised

At the end of this unit students should be able to:
- understand more about the requirements of writing an academic essay;
- produce a clear outline.

Task 1 Basic principles of essay writing

Lead in by asking students to discuss, in pairs, their worst and best essay-writing experience. After a brief round-up, elicit different types of essay and write students' suggestions on the board. Then ask students to compare the ideas on the board with the list in Task 1. Ask students to work in small groups, saying what they understand each type to be.

1.1 Small group work

Set this activity, asking students to underline the words in the essay titles that helped them identify the essay type. You may need to spend some time clarifying the different essay types in a plenary session at the end of the activity.

Title	Type
Using your <u>personal experience</u>, <u>describe</u> a particularly interesting cultural encounter.	descriptive + personal experience
What are <u>the main arguments for and against</u> the implementation of very high rates of taxation?	argument
<u>How good do you think</u> the author is at creating the characters in this story? <u>Analyse</u> the characterisation and give examples.	evaluative + analytical
<u>The most efficient</u> form of transport is the train. Discuss.	evaluative
Using the statistics in the accompanying table, write an <u>analytical description</u> of the rise in the number of British households.	analytical + descriptive
The European Union is already far too big. Discuss.	argument
Learning a language is <u>one of the best forms</u> of educational activity. <u>Do you agree</u>?	evaluative + argument

1.2 Small group work

Answers:
- a) introduction
- b) body
- c) conclusion

1.3 Pairwork/small group work

In order to prepare the way for the task, you could copy a short 'model' essay onto card (one per pair/small group), cut it up into paragraphs and ask the pairs/groups to put the pieces into the correct order. The students could then use the essay as a concrete example on which to base their discussions of Exercise 1.3 questions. Encourage students to make notes on their discussions. They can use these in a plenary session at the end of the activity in which they feed back to the class.

1.4 Individual work/pairwork

According to the needs of your students, you might need to pre-teach the following:

- essay outline;
- edit (a piece of writing);
- source material;
- to draft (a piece of writing);
- proofread (a piece of writing);
- paraphrase.

Ask students to complete the questionnaire and then compare their answers with a partner's.

Task 2 Analysing the essay question

2.1 Pairwork

This activity could be tackled in a number of ways according to the needs of your students. You could ask pairs of students to explain the differences in meaning between the instruction words.

Alternatively, you could use the photocopiable vocabulary grid below, copying the larger version on page 72, an giving one card to each student in your class. Ask each student to read his/her card and look up any words they are unsure of. Then ask the students to stand up and move around the room, teaching their word to another member of the group, who then reciprocates by teaching his/her word. When both students have finished explaining, the pair swap cards and then each student looks for a new partner to teach his/her word to.

Identify	Analyse	Describe	Comment on
Describe items that belong to a particular category.	Examine in detail by dividing up. Identify the main points.	Give the main features, characteristics or events.	Identify the main issues and give an informed opinion.
Compare	**Discuss**	**Evaluate**	**Exemplify**
Describe the main elements of two or more things to show how they are similar. Possibly explain the consequences of the similarities.	Look at the most important aspects of something in a balanced way, i.e., advantages and disadvantages; for and against.	Assess how important or useful something is. It is likely to include both positive and negative points.	Show what something is like, using examples.

Task 3 Brainstorming ideas

Explain to the students that once they have understood the essay task that has been set, the next stage is to brainstorm ideas on the topic of the essay.

3.1 Individual work

Model free writing for your students on the board, explaining that they should keep their pens/pencils on the paper at all times and that they should write continuously for two minutes. Tell them that this is possible as they are not expected to edit their ideas but simply write whatever comes into their heads on the topic of transporting goods by road. When the students have done this, put them to work in small groups, comparing their texts for similar ideas or themes. Have a brief plenary session in which you collect some ideas on the board.

3.2 Small group work

Lead in by asking students to shut their eyes and picture a lorry in the middle of a town. Elicit whether the image the students saw was a positive one, e.g., a lorry delivering medicines to a hospital; a negative one, e.g., a lorry stuck in a traffic-jam with black smoke coming out of its exhaust; or a more neutral image. Introduce the topic of banning lorries from towns and cities, asking students to think of anything that comes into their heads on this topic and then sharing ideas with the rest of their group. Provide an OHT and pen for each group if you would like the students to share their ideas in a brief plenary at the end of the task.

Before moving on to the next task, you could hold a brief plenary session in which you ask the students whether they preferred brainstorming individually through free writing, or bouncing ideas off each other in a group.

Task 4 Organising your ideas

Before setting Exercise 4.1, ask students to work in small groups analysing the question. Refer the students back to Exercises 1.1 and 2.1 in Unit 1.

4.1 Individual work

Set this activity as individual work, explaining that after five minutes the small groups will re-form to exchange ideas.

4.2 Small group work

This activity will probably go better if you provide students with A1 paper and some post-it notes, one for each idea. This allows the groups to move ideas around, before fixing their position on the A1 paper and connecting the ideas together with arrows. Allow 15–20 minutes for this step. Each group should present its essay-poster in a plenary session at the end of the activity and the essay-posters can then form a wall display.

Possible questions your students might address are:
  a) Who suffers from traffic congestion?
  b) What problems are caused by traffic congestion?
  c) What are the possible solutions?
  d) What are the best solutions?
  e) Why are these the best solutions?
  f) Which solutions are not effective? Why?

If you feel some peer evaluation would be useful at this juncture, elicit some criteria for feedback on the plans from the group and write these criteria on the board. Provide each small group with post-it notes of a different colour to the first set and assign them the task of working together to evaluate another small group's plan. Ask each group to choose one member to act as a scribe who writes the group's comments on the post-it notes and then sticks them onto the relevant plan.

Unit 2 – Getting started

At the end of this unit students will:
• be better equipped to start writing an essay;
• understand how to write a thesis statement;
• have ideas on how to make the introduction interesting for the reader.

Task 1 What to include

The purpose of this task is to encourage students to select relevant information and to prioritise the selected information before organising it in a logical way.

1.1 Individual work/small group work

First, ask students to evaluate the importance of the points individually and then ask them to discuss their ideas in small groups. There may be some variation in answers, depending on the argument students wish to pursue.
  a) I
  b) U – this could be background information, but should not take up a major part of the essay.
  c) NI
  e) I – the students should be encouraged to see that it is not so much a list that is required as an evaluation of these solutions.
  f) U/NI – the students should be encouraged to carry out research to find supporting evidence. They should probably broaden the scope of the essay beyond their immediate surroundings.
  g) I – arguments for or against various solutions should form the main body of the essay.

1.2 Individual work

In order to help students understand the principles of ordering information, it might be worth modelling the first half of an essay on the topic. Elicit which of the items mentioned in the list in Exercise 1.1 would come first and why (e.g., definition so that the writer establishes common ground with the reader, etc.). Elicit what would come next and why, and so on. Then set the remainder of the task as individual work. Ask students to compare their answers in pairs.

Task 2 Information gathering

2.1 Pairwork

Encourage the pairs to think of types of information source. To help them in this task, draw their attention to the visuals.

Possible answers, depending on availability, include:

- books
- newspaper articles
- journal articles
- websites
- documentaries

2.2 Individual work

This exercise offers the opportunity for students to evaluate their strengths and weaknesses, so the answers will vary from student to student.

2.3 Plenary

The plenary provides you with the opportunity to find out which skills areas worry your students the most and this information could provide a rationale for some remedial work on areas of perceived weakness.

Task 3 Arousing interest: The introduction

As a lead-in to Task 3 you could photocopy a number of introductions to essays on topics with which your students are familiar and ask them to choose their favourite introduction, giving reasons for their choice.

3.1 Individual work/pairwork

Answer: a)

3.2 Individual work/pairwork/plenary

While the students are writing, circulate and correct any language errors in their work. At the end of the task, collect some examples of first sentences for one of the essay topics on the board. Then ask students to work in pairs, discussing which first sentence they prefer and why. Elicit preferences and reasons in a brief plenary.

Task 4 Writing a thesis statement

4.1 Individual work

If your students are unfamiliar with the notion of a controlling idea, you should model the first example on the board.

Answers:
  a) HOW the criminal justice system functions in my country.
  b) The QUESTIONS left unanswered by the Big Bang Theory.
  c) TWO SOLUTIONS to coping with sea-level rises:
  - education on the effects of sea-level rises
  - accurate forecasting of its hazards

4.2 Individual work

Draw students' attention to the language issues related to the essay organisation signposting section:

a) Use of impersonal subject, e.g., This essay starts by discussing definitions of... (NOT 'I will start...')

b) Choice between *will/present simple*, e.g., This essay will first outline...and then it will discuss... or This essay first outlines...and then it discusses...

c) Typical sentence structures, e.g., In the first section, X is defined. (prepositional phrase + passive voice) or The essay first defines X. ('The essay' as subject + active voice)

Ask students to use a variety of structures to complete Exercise 4.2.

4.3 Individual work

Model this task for your students, possibly taking two different views about possible solutions to the problems of traffic congestion and showing how the different views would result in different thesis statements. Circulate and correct your students' work where necessary.

4.4 Individual work

Return to the two examples you modelled in Exercise 4.3 and show your students how the signposting statements would differ due to differences in the thesis statements. Circulate and correct your students' work where necessary.

Example answer:
There is growing agreement that the way to control the congestion that ruins our towns and cities is to tax the motorist. This essay will argue for the use of various taxation policies to address the traffic congestion problem in Britain, using London and Edinburgh as examples. It will first evaluate congestion charging as one possible solution, and then discuss the effect of motorway tolls.

Task 5 An effective introduction

5.1 Small group work

You could photocopy the sentences of the introduction onto card, one copy per small group, and ask the students to work in their groups to re-form the introduction.

Alternatively, you could turn this activity into a running dictation by cutting up one copy of the sentences and blu-tacking the sentences onto one wall of your classroom. Ask students to work in pairs, one playing the role of runner and the other that of scribe. Move a line of desks to the far end of the classroom opposite the wall with the sentences on it. Ask the scribes to sit behind these desks. Clear the other furniture to the side of the room to provide a clear path for the runners. Give each scribe five strips of paper to write the five sentences on. Tell the runners to run to the other end of the room, read a sentence and memorise as much of it as possible, including the punctuation, and then run back to their partner and dictate. The scribe notes down the dictation. The runner returns to memorise the next part, and so on. When all the sentences have been written down by the scribe, the pair should organise the five sentences into a general-specific introduction. The pairs who finish quickest can then compare the accuracy of their dictation with the sentences given in the course book.

Answers:
  e), b), a), d), c)

5.2 Pairwork

Answers:
  a) Statements e), b) and a) are general and give important background information to help the reader understand the context of the problem.
  b) Statement c) is the thesis statement. The essay will follow the order outlined in the thesis statement and will focus on evaluating solutions.
  c) The body of the essay will require at least six paragraphs as sentence d) lists four direct problems and two knock-on problems. The essay will probably be organised as a Problem–Solution–Evaluation text.

5.3 & 5.4 Individual work/pairwork

Ask students to apply the criteria in Exercise 5.3 to the introduction given in Exercise 5.4 and make notes in their course books.

Answers:
Your students should notice that the thesis statement fails to explain the focus of the essay, though it can be inferred that the essay will examine the effects of GM foods on people's environment and their health.

5.5 Individual work/pairwork

Take in and correct the introductions. Ask students to prepare a corrected copy of their introductions for a peer evaluation session in the next class. Encourage the students to refer back to the criteria listed in Exercise 5.3 to help with the task of evaluating the introductions.

Unit 3 – The body of the essay

At the end of this unit students will:
- have a clear idea how to structure the main part of an academic essay;
- know how to plan and write effective paragraphs.

Task 1 Paragraph organisation

1.1 Individual work/plenary

Answers:
  a) true
  b) false
  c) true
  d) false – examples, figures and statistics are three types of supporting material. There are other types too, depending on your discipline, e.g., paraphrasing/quoting opinions given in authoritative sources
  e) false – as noted above, support can be given through quoting other authorities, but you can also paraphrase
  f) true

1.2 Individual work
Answer:

1 The first episode in the Coca-Cola story is an important part of the rise of capitalism in the United States of America. Towards the end of the nineteenth century, America gradually began to transform itself from a nation of farmers to a city-based, industrialised society. The industrial revolution was epitomised by new communications and the arrival and spread of the railways. This produced a new kind of capitalism, a distinctive American variety where the ethos centred firmly on the image of individual immigrant struggle. The world of US business was on its way.

2 One of the most important changes that helped business success was population growth. The American population almost doubled in size between 1880 and 1910, a large part of which was new immigrants from Europe and the rest of the world. Success came from ambition and hard work and anybody could make large amounts of money provided they worked hard enough. Helped by the success of some, immigrants flocked to the USA. By 1890, there were already over 4,000 American millionaires and Andrew Carnegie, who had made a fortune from railways and iron and steel, was spreading the "Gospel of Wealth".

3 There were, however, some disadvantages to the new business environment. In many parts of the USA, there was more than an element of the Wild West. Conmen, thieves and swindlers came to the new towns that were appearing, looking for suitable victims. A second major disadvantage was that Coke was originally a patent medicine and only about two per cent of the medicines produced ever became well-known – most inventors and salesmen failed miserably. Thirdly, although large profits could be made from all kinds of medicines, many of which often cost almost nothing to produce, by the late 1880s the market for medicines was already saturated. Patent medicines, therefore, were not an easy commercial area to break into.

4 Another important aspect of the story is that the world of medicine was not advanced at this time. Nineteenth-century American doctors were not numerous, nor were they very good (anaesthetics were still to be invented and some of the primitive methods used by the medical profession were terrifying, killing more patients than they saved). This was the reason why many people turned to alternative remedies, the so-called patent medicines, to solve their health problems. By the end of the century, there were thousands of cures on offer for every imaginable ailment, from the common cold to malaria, all of which required extensive advertising in newspapers and public places to promote their superior values over their competitors.

5 To conclude, it is not surprising that many would-be tycoons were attracted by the rising numbers of consumers, and that the field of patent medicines was an attractive starting point for some. In 1869, Dr John Pemberton, a Georgia pharmacist, had moved to Atlanta searching to make his fortune by the discovery of the perfect patent cure. In 1886, after long years of research, he finally launched his new invention. It was into this very crowded and over-competitive market that Coca-Cola was to emerge as a highly successful product.

Task 2 Linking words and phrases

2.1 Individual work
Answers:
Firstly = The <u>first</u> episode
Secondly = <u>One</u> of the most important changes
Thirdly = There were, <u>however</u>, some <u>disadvantages</u>
Fourthly = <u>Another</u> important aspect
Finally = <u>To conclude</u>

2.2 Individual work/pairwork
Answers:
Showing similarity – **in the same way**
Comparing or contrasting – **on the other hand**
Adding something – **equally important; another important aspect**
Giving reasons
Showing cause and effect – **as a result; therefore**
Giving an example – **as shown by; for instance; like**

After you have clarified the answers to the question, you could ask students to add to the linkers in each list by brainstorming with a partner.

Task 3 The topic sentence and supporting sentences

3.1 Pairwork
Answer: c)

3.2 Small group work
Answer:

Example A is a better-formed paragraph because it develops the idea stated in the topic sentence. In contrast, Example B tends to digress from the topic sentence statement (challenges for incoming families) into an argument about the human rights of incomers.

3.3 Individual work
Responses here will vary. It is a good idea to take this work in and check it.

Task 4 Organising an essay

4.1 Individual work/pairwork/small group work

Paragraph begins	Topic	Order
Another important aspect of the story is that the world of medicine was not advanced at this time.	the world of medicine	4
There were, however, some disadvantages to the new business environment.	disadvantages to the business environment	3
To conclude, it is not surprising that many would-be tycoons were attracted by the rising numbers of consumers and that the field of patent medicines was an attractive starting point for some.	the field of patent medicines was an attractive one for would-be tycoons	5
One of the most important changes that helped business success was population growth.	population growth	2
The first episode in the Coca-Cola story is an important part of the rise of capitalism in the United States of America.	the rise of capitalism	1

4.2, 4.3 & 4.4 Pairwork/individual work
After the discussion task in Exercise 4.2, the remaining two exercises could be set for homework.

Unit 4 – Summaries and conclusions

At the end of this unit the students will:
- have a clear idea of how to finish an academic essay with a successful conclusion.

Task 1 Restating the thesis

1.1 Pairwork
Answers:

Original	Synonym
lack of	insufficient
consequences	impact
travellers	commuters
major point	main focus
discussed	explored

1.2 Individual work/pairwork
Possible answer:

In conclusion, this essay has argued that insufficient investment in Britain's public transport system has had a negative impact on commuters in this country.

Task 2 Organising the concluding paragraph

2.1 Individual work/pairwork
Ask students to do this task individually and then compare answers with a partner.

Answer:
b), a), d), c), e)

Task 3 Finish with a clear statement

3.1 Pairwork
Possible answers:
  a) Fast food and its impact on health in Britain. Possible title = Discuss the impact of fast food on health in Britain.
  b) In a similar vein to the introduction, the conclusion states that fast food plays a role in Britons' unhealthy dietary habits. The conclusion adds the idea, however, that increased consumption of fast food is an effect of changes in lifestyle and it is these that underlie the development of an increasingly unhealthy Britain.

3.2 Individual work
This activity could be set for homework.

3.3 Pairwork
Possible answers:
  Advantages:
  You know the destination of your essay.
  Your conclusion matches your thesis statement.
  Disadvantages:
  As you are writing, you may change your argument. If you forget to change your conclusion, it will not match your thesis statement.

Task 4 Lecturer expectations

4.1 Individual work
This activity could be set for homework. It might form the basis of a tutorial if these feature in your course.

Unit 5 – Academic style and register

At the end of this unit students will:
- be more familiar with the language of essays and able to identify some of the features of academic style;
- have practised using formal, objective language.

Task 1 Formal or informal register?

Lead in by focusing the students' attention on the visuals and eliciting the differences between the formal and informal situation.

1.1 & 1.2 Individual work/pairwork
Answers:

Feature	Informal/spoken examples	Formal/written examples
Use of contractions *isn't, don't,* etc.	contractions used, e.g., *which'd*	full forms used, e.g., *which, would*
Use of fillers *Well, …er* etc.	used, e.g., *well, um, …er*	not used
Use of passive voice	active voice preferred, e.g., *you could look at how human beings adapt themselves to the environment, that's human*	more frequent, e.g., *two main branches may be distinguished*
Impersonal and objective	—	Non-use of personal pronouns, e.g., *I; the reader is not mentioned*
Personal and subjective	Use of personal pronouns, e.g., *I think*; addresses listener as *you*	—
Punctuation	Uses intonation	Uses punctuation
Imprecise language	e.g., *some sort of mix of physical and social sciences*	Avoids imprecision
Conciseness	Uses a clause to express an idea, e.g., *how they interact together*	Prefers concise forms, e.g., noun phrases for an idea, e.g. *the interrelation of these features*

1.3 Pairwork
Answers:
  a) I   g) I
  b) F   h) I
  c) F   i) F
  d) I   j) I
  e) F   k) I
  f) I   l) F

Task 2 Cautious language

2.1 Individual work
Answer:
  Hedging language

2.2 Pairwork
Answers:

A Some colleges and universities in this country <u>appear to have</u> large numbers of international students.

B <u>It could be argued that</u>, instead of coming here, international students should study in their own country.

C This <u>would seem to be</u> a misapplication of government policy.

D <u>To a certain extent</u>, this <u>may</u> be true.

E Erlichman's findings <u>suggest</u> that the amount of independent study <u>might</u> be directly related to higher performance levels.

F <u>Evidence indicates that</u> inflation will <u>probably</u> not rise next year.

G The survey <u>tends to indicate</u> that English schoolchildren are <u>apparently</u> not in favour of learning more foreign languages.

H There are <u>undoubtedly</u> situations where this <u>would seem to be</u> the only <u>possible</u> solution.

Hedging feature	Example
hedging verbs, e.g., *appear to be*	Some colleges…<u>appear</u> to have… This would <u>seem</u> to be… Erlichman's findings <u>suggest</u> …this <u>would seem to be</u>… The survey <u>tends to indicate</u> that…
Use of modal verbs	This <u>would seem</u> to be… …this <u>may</u> be true… the amount of independent study <u>might</u> be…
Qualifying expressions	<u>It could be argued that</u>… <u>To a certain extent</u>,… <u>Evidence indicates that</u>…
Adjectives and adverbs	…inflation will <u>probably</u> not rise… English schoolchildren are <u>apparently</u> not in favour… There are <u>undoubtedly</u> situations where… …the only <u>possible</u> solution.
Set expressions	

Task 3 Register in use

3.1 & 3.2 Individual work/pairwork
Ask students to work through the task, compare with a partner and then look at the original text in Unit 3, Exercise 2.1 together.

Possible answers:
A <u>massive</u> *change* – <u>one which really helped business – was more people arriving</u> *in the USA.* <u>There were two times as many people who got here</u> *between 1880 and 1910 and* <u>lots of them came from</u> <u>all sorts of different places like</u> *Europe. If* <u>you</u> *wanted to be successful* <u>you had to work really hard;</u> *however,* <u>you</u> *could get rich quickly if* <u>you did this.</u> <u>Lots of</u> *immigrants* <u>made it</u> *and because of this,* <u>lots</u> *more* <u>wannabe millionaires</u> <u>turned up</u> *in the* <u>US</u>*. By 1890, America* <u>maybe had around</u> *4,000 millionaires. One of the* <u>best</u> *was Andrew Carnegie, who* <u>got rich</u> *through* <u>trains and</u> *iron and steel. His message was called the "Gospel of Wealth".*

3.3 Pairwork/individual work

Ask students to work in pairs to identify inappropriate language and places where hedging would be appropriate.

Model answer:

A further kind of useful alternative fuel is electricity. At present, this would not seem to be a very efficient fuel, because the technology is somewhat limited; however, it may be argued that recent advances in the production of electric cars could make this a reality in the future. Cars powered with electricity tend to release little or no emissions, so to maximise this benefit it would be advisable to encourage consumers to switch to buying electric cars. Changing consumer preferences may take some time.

Unit 6 – Guidelines for the future

At the end of this unit the students will:
- understand the editing and redrafting processes in essay writing;
- have a clearer understanding of what lecturers expect from a piece of academic writing.

Task 1 Things to remember

1.1 Individual work
Answers will vary from student to student.

Task 2 Redrafting

2.1 Plenary
Answers:
   a) probably a minimum of two
   b) • relevance of the answer to the title;
      • logical organisation of ideas;
      • substantiation of claims;
      • accurate paraphrasing;
      • adequate referencing and bibliography;
      • accurate language.

2.2 Pairwork/small group work/plenary
Possible answers:

Redrafting: things to work on:	Considerations
paragraphs	• the right structure • each paragraph has a main idea • paragraphs are in the right order
grammar	• articles • sentence grammar • word order • accurate link words
length of essay	respect the instructions
vocabulary	accurate use of technical terms
argument	• evidence supports the claim made in a paragraph • the main claims support the thesis statement • the thesis statement is echoed by the summary sentence in the conclusion • the argument is relevant to the question set
sources	• accurate quotations • accurate paraphrasing • adequate and accurate referencing • accurate bibliography
formal style	• impersonal, objective tone • formal vocabulary, e.g., latinate • full forms • avoids colloquialisms and idiomatic language

Task 3 How to get a better mark

3.1 Pairwork
Ask students to discuss in pairs the answers to this task.

Answers:
   c), f)

3.2 Individual work/plenary
Ask students to make a note of their own examples. Then elicit some of these in a brief plenary session.

3.3 Individual work
Answers:

Marking criteria	Mark (%)
ideas generally not made clear and often irrelevant; weak paragraphs; small range of vocabulary; grammatical structure is very limited	40–49
ideas generally clear but not always very relevant; some lack of paragraphing; limited range of vocabulary; limited grammatical structure at times	50–59
lacks any satisfactory organisation or development of ideas; vocabulary use very weak; unsatisfactory use of grammatical structure; generally fails to meet the required pass standard	30–39
excellent text organisation; clear paragraphs with well-expressed ideas; wide range of vocabulary; good use of grammatical structure	70+
good text organisation with generally relevant ideas; adequate range of vocabulary and grammatical structure	60–69

Task 4 A model essay

4.1 Individual work
Answers:

Essay title: <u>Discuss</u> the problems associated with urban overcrowding and <u>evaluate</u> possible solutions.

4.2 Individual work/pairwork
Ask students to work through the questions on their own and then compare their answers with a partner's.

Answers:
a) The writer arouses interest in the reader by underlining the global nature and actuality of the problem.
b) The purpose of this essay is to <u>identify</u> solutions to some of these problems of urban overcrowding and attempt to <u>evaluate</u> their feasibility.

4.3 Individual work
This task lends itself to homework. After students have worked on the task individually, they should compare notes with a partner.

Answers:

Paragraph 1
Topic sentence key words: Urban overcrowding = has become a global phenomenon
Support examples and evidence: Rise of megacities – around 20 million population = important trend in last 20 years, e.g., New York

Paragraph 2
Topic sentence key words: Reasons for megacities' growth: economic security + improved social conditions
Support examples and evidence: Cities develop as economic centres, e.g., post-2nd WW megacities: Sydney, Sao Paulo + Frankfurt; Tokyo – expanded in line with the city's economic growth

Paragraph 3
Topic sentence key words: No. 1 problem = poverty + inability of developing countries to cope with high population density in cities
Support examples and evidence: Rural → urban migration: live in shanty towns on edge of city. Problems: unsanitary living conditions; infectious diseases.↓ access to health care + education

Paragraph 4
Topic sentence key words: Two main solutions: both relocate urban population outside cities.
Support examples and evidence: 1st solution – resettlement, e.g., Shanghai housing resettlement project – successful → social + economic benefits BUT not address problem of urban sprawl.

Paragraph 5
Topic sentence key words: 2nd solution = relocation of employers to rural areas
Support examples and evidence: e.g., brownfield sites in rural areas become business parks – successful in Canada & UK BUT:
1) requires long-term investment by government as people will only relocate if have better housing, education, transport, etc.
2) threat to rural environment according to environmentalists.

4.4 Pairwork

Answers:

   a) paragraphs 1 & 2

   b) paragraphs 4 & 5

   c) paragraph 3

4.5 Pairwork

Answers:

   a) suggestion that long-term measures would benefit the lives of all city dwellers

   b) generalises about the type of solutions that would work well, i.e., long-term ones

4.6 Individual work/pairwork

Ask students to work alone, underlining examples of assertive language first. They should compare with a partner and then work as a pair, adding cautious language to the text. Answers will vary from pair to pair.

If you have a large class, you could give half the pairs a photocopy on OHT of the first half of the text, and half a photocopy on OHT of the second half of the text. When each pair has identified overly assertive language and rewritten using cautious language on the OHT, the pairs could be asked to present their new version to the class, explaining why the changes were made.

Task 5 Write an essay outline

5.1 Individual work

This task could be set for homework as students would benefit from carrying out research in order to substantiate their claims.

5.2 Small group work

Ask students to present their outline plans in small groups. Encourage the other group members to give feedback using the set of criteria given in Task 5.

Identify	Analyse	Describe	Comment on
Describe items that belong to a particular category.	Examine in detail by dividing up. Identify the main points.	Give the main features, characteristics or events.	Identify the main issues and give an informed opinion.

Compare	Discuss	Evaluate	Exemplify
Describe the main elements of two or more things to show how they are similar. Possibly explain the consequences of the similarities.	Look at the most important aspects of something in a balanced way, i.e., advantages and disadvantages; for and against.	Assess how important or useful something is. It is likely to include both positive and negative points.	Show what something is like, using examples.

Scientific Writing

Unit 1 – Structure and schedule

At the end of this unit students should be able to:
- structure a report and include appropriate scientific report sections;
- organise their time appropriately.

Task 1 Organising a scientific report

1.1 Pairwork/small group work

As a lead-in, focus students on the visuals and ask them to work in pairs discussing what the five sections of a scientific paper are. Having elicited the answer to a), ask students to work in small groups to complete the table.

Sections	Questions
1 Introduction	What was the theoretical background of the experiment? What was the aim of the experiment?
2 Materials & methods	What did I do?
3 Results	What did I find out?
4 Discussion	What do my results mean?
5 Bibliography	What references did I use?

1.2 Plenary

Ask students to give reasons for their answers. If the students have had experience of writing scientific reports, ask them to give examples from their own writing.

Task 2 Organising your time

2.1 Individual work/pairwork

Ask the students to work individually, putting the stages in order and then comparing their answers with a partner's. This should take about ten minutes. Encourage students to share their ideas in a brief plenary.

    1 = l) Complete practical laboratory work
    2 = g) Write first draft of the *Material and Methods*

    3 = m) Write first draft of the *Results* (do calculations, draw up tables, graphs, chart)
    4 = h) Research background information
    5 = j) Start *Bibliography*
    6 = f) Write first draft of the *Discussion*
    7 = b) Write first draft of the *Introduction*
    8 = k) Give first draft to another student to review using list of 'Points to check'.
    9 = i) Meet with another student to discuss peer review (have a writing conference)
    10= a) Revise first draft
    11= c) Hand in revised draft

Note: There are two extra steps (d) and (e) that the students do not need to use.

2.2 & 2.3 Individual work/small group work

Ask students to fill in the table individually and then to compare their answers in small groups. Answers will vary.

Suggested timetable:

Time-frame	Activity	Reason
Day 0	Complete practical laboratory work	Lab work is fun!
Day 1	Write first draft of *Material and Methods*. Write first draft of *Results* (do calculations, draw up tables, graphs, chart).	The laboratory work is still fresh in your mind and you need time to complete all the parts of the report before submission.
Day 2	Research background information. Start Bibliography. Write first draft of the *Discussion*. Write first draft of the *Introduction*.	You need to know the background literature before writing the *Discussion* and *Introduction*. Writing your Bibliography as you go along will save time, and errors, at the end.
Day 3	Revise first draft.	Taking a break between writing the first draft and revising it allows you to view it more critically/objectively.
Day 4	Give first draft to a classmate to review using list of 'Points to check'.	Peer review can be helpful.
Day 5	Meet with classmate to discuss peer review (have a writing conference).	Discussion with your classmate allows you to explain what you intended and for your reviewer to provide feedback.
Day 6	Revise first draft.	Revise as necessary, remembering that you do not have to include all the reviewer's suggestions.
Day 7	Hand in revised draft.	Submitting on time avoids loss of credit through late submission.

Remember, you can adjust the timeframe according to your own deadlines.

Unit 2 – The *Materials and Methods* section

At the end of this unit students will know:
- what to include in the *Materials and Methods* section of a report;
- how and why to write in the passive voice.

Task 1 What do I include?

1.1 Small group work
Ask each group to choose a secretary whose role is to make a note of the main points raised in the discussion. The remaining students should discuss the two questions.

Possible answers include:

Include ...	Do not include ...
• temperature (air, water); • volume of materials used; • mass of materials used; • concentrations of solutions; • pH; • type of microscopy; • sampling techniques; • species name of organism; • age of organisms used; • size of organisms used.	Information that is common knowledge to the scientific audience reading the report, e.g.: • detailed descriptions of conventional laboratory glassware; • detailed descriptions of conventional laboratory techniques.

1.2 Plenary
Ask each group secretary to report back on the discussion and collect ideas on the board.

1.3 Individual work
Answers: b + c

Task 2 How do I write a good *Materials and Methods* section?

One possible lead-in is to focus students' attention on the visual and ask them to identify which document is a report and which document is a laboratory schedule.

2.1 Individual work
Refer the students back to the example report and schedule. Ask them to complete the cloze individually and then compare with a partner.

Answers:
Laboratory schedules are usually written in the underline{imperative} as a list of instructions. However, when you write your report, you must summarise what you did in full underline{sentences} and well-developed underline{paragraphs}. You will usually write in the underline{past} tense and use the underline{passive} voice.

2.2 Plenary

Ask students to think about any reports they have written previously. Did these reports have a similar style?

Then ask the students to consider the questions asked in the book.
Answers:
  a) A schedule is a set of instructions to follow (a protocol) in order to complete an analytical procedure. A report explains what you did and why.
  b) Paragraphs are used to separate and organise ideas and to provide clarity.
  c) The passive is common as it focuses the reader's attention on underline{what} was done rather than on underline{who} did it.

2.3 Plenary
Answer: b)

Task 3 Using the passive

3.1 Individual work
The object in the active sentence, *the analysis*, becomes the underline{subject} in the passive sentence. The subject in the active sentence, *John*, changes position in the passive sentence as it comes underline{after} the main verb and is introduced with underline{by}.

3.2 Individual work
In the active sentence above, the two objects are: underline{the caterpillars} and underline{one dose}. One or the other can become the subject in the *passive* sentence.

3.3 Individual work
Answers:

Past simple

The plant was taken.	The plants were taken.
A pot was made.	The pots were made.
The image was shown.	The images were shown.

Past perfect

The solution had been shaken.	The solutions had been shaken.
The animal had been fed.	The animals had been fed.
The mixture had been kept.	The mixtures had been kept.

Past continuous

A record was being made.	Records were being made.
An attachment was being fitted.	Attachments were being fitted.
The result was being analysed.	The results were being analysed.

3.4 Small group work
Focus students' attention on the tutor's feedback at the end of the *Materials and Methods* section. Ask each group of students to work through the text three times, first identifying how to focus the reader on the method, second looking at improving the paragraphing and finally underlining all the nouns. The students should make a note of their discussions.

3.5 Individual work/pairwork
This activity could be set as homework.

Possible answer:
Field work recordings were started on 12 February 2005, and ended on 12 March 2005. A digital camera was used to record the animals found on the beach and animals were marked with quick-drying, non-toxic paint. Recordings of environmental conditions, including temperature, salinity and substrate, were being made at the same time.

Laboratory experiments were begun at the same time as the field work. Each day ten animals were collected from the beach and placed in controlled conditions in the laboratory until experiments began.

The apparatus was set up as shown in Figure 1 and one crab was placed in each specimen tube. By the time an experiment started, the crabs had been acclimatised for at least two days and had been fed daily. Food had been prepared in advance.

At the end of each experiment, a digital camera was used to record the animals' appearance. Photographs taken at the beach had been

printed for comparison. The results <u>were being analysed</u> continuously.
Results <u>were analysed</u> using statistical tests.

For your feedback session on this task, the exercise on the following page can be photocopied onto card and cut up. Ask students to rearrange the paragraphs in the correct order and then decide whether the missing verbs should be active or passive and what the tense should be.

Paragraph order spells: FIELD
Missing verbs are underlined in the text above.

L

At the end of each experiment, a digital camera _____(use) to record the animals' appearance. Photographs taken at the beach had been printed for comparison. The results _____ (analyse) continuously.

D

Results _____ (analyse) using statistical tests.

I

Laboratory experiments _____ (begin) at the same time as the field work. Each day ten animals were collected from the beach and placed in controlled conditions in the laboratory until experiments _____ (begin).

F

Field work recordings _____ (start) on 12 February 2005 and ended on 12 March 2005. A digital camera was used to record the animals found on the beach and animals were marked with quick-drying, non-toxic paint. Recordings of environmental conditions, including temperature, salinity and substrate, _____ (make) at the same time.

E

The apparatus was set up as shown in Figure 1 and one crab was placed in each specimen tube. By the time an experiment started, the crabs had been acclimatised for at least 2 days and _____ (feed) daily. Food had been prepared in advance.

Unit 3 – The *Results* section

At the end of this unit students will know:
- what to include in the *Results* section;
- how to present and describe tables and figures;
- how to write up results.

Task 1 What to include

1.1 Pairwork

Answers:

Clockwise from left: pie chart; histogram; line graph; table.

1.2 Pairwork

Answers:
a) A figure is a graphical representation of the data, a table is the data itself.
b) Tables/figures should be included as they clarify/simplify results.
c) Table – title above; figure – title below.
d) Labels, titles.

Task 2 Preparing tables and graphs

2.1 Pairwork

Answers:
a) • Table 1 lists points of comparison across the top of the table and species down the side. Table 2 does the reverse.
   • Table 1 gives units of measurement for the points of comparison, while Table 2 does not.
   • Table 1 gives the date when the data were collected; Table 2 does not.
   • Table 2 uses abbreviations inconsistently, e.g., Av./Aver.
b) Table 1
c) It would <u>not</u> be better to show this data in a graph. It would be better in a table.

2.2 Small group work

Possible answers:
- Data for a particular characteristic are arranged vertically, rather than horizontally.
- Each column heading is followed by the units.
- Numbers in a column are aligned to the right.
- Only acceptable abbreviations are used.
- The table has a number (Arabic) and a title.

- The title is complete and allows the reader to understand the essence of the table without referring to the text.

2.3 Small group work

Answers:

Strengths	Weaknesses
• Most of the data are accurately represented.	• The independent data is on the y-axis • Not all axes are labelled • Spelling error in the title • Data not always accurately represented

2.4 & 2.5 Individual work/pairwork

Ask students to discuss the questions in pairs and then draw their graphs individually. When they have finished, they should compare their work with their partner.

Answer:

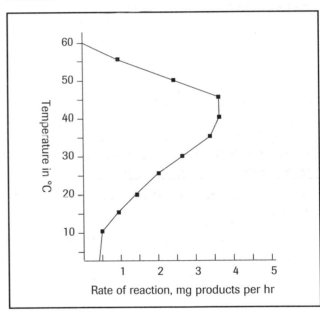

Task 3 Writing the text of the *Results* section

Ask students to look at the sample paragraph and find examples of:
a) past tense verbs in the active voice;
b) an important finding;
c) reference to a table or figure;
d) specific details of the data that support the finding.

Answers:
   a) varied/was/increased/decreased
   b) Oxygen production varied depending on the pH of the solution
   c) (Figure 1)
   d) At pH 2, oxygen production was 3ml, whereas at pH 7 it increased to a maximum of 6ml. At pH values above 7, oxygen production decreased and was at a minimum of 1ml at pH 10.

3.1 Pairwork
Ask students to work with a partner identifying findings and supporting evidence.

3.2 Pairwork/small group work
Students follow the instructions in the course book.

Unit 4 – Writing numbers and abbreviations

At the end of this unit students will know:
- when to use numerals and when to spell numbers in scientific reports;
- how to use very large and very small numbers;
- the conventions for using abbreviations.

Task 1 Writing numbers

1.1 Pairwork
Put students into pairs. Ask them to read through the guidelines to find examples of numerals, ordinals, fractions and decimal forms and then to check with their partners.

Possible answers:
   a) a numeral = 2
   b) an ordinal = seventh
   c) a fraction = a third
   d) a decimal form = 0.5

Then ask students to explain the terms 'numeral' and 'ordinal' to their partners without looking back at the course book. When they have finished this, they should check their work against the explanations given in the course book.

a numeral = used to express *quantities* and *mathematical relationships.*
an ordinal = number that conveys order or rank

Then elicit explanations of 'fraction' and 'decimal form'.

1.2 Individual work/pairwork
Ask students to work through the exercise individually, referring back to the guidelines to help them. They should compare their answers with a partner and be prepared to explain them.

Answers:
   a) iii   d) i
   b) v   e) ii
   c) iv

1.3 Individual work
Answers:
   b) Five Gammarus were placed in 50 ml of 0%, 50% and 100% seawater solutions.
   c) The animals were collected at Swansea Bay and one half were divided between three 50 ml pots.
   d) After washing twice in buffer, the tissue was immersed in 2% osmium tetroxide in 0.25 M phosphate buffer, for 1 hr.

Task 2 Common scientific abbreviations

2.1 Plenary
If you think your class would be familiar with most of the abbreviations, this activity could be turned into a competition, with the two halves of the class competing to find the full forms of the abbreviations. When this is finished, ask the students to complete the exercise in their course books in writing.

Alternatively, if you think your students will tend to be unfamiliar with the abbreviations, this activity could be turned into a vocabulary snowball, using the photocopiable page at the end of the module. This should be copied onto card and cut up. Give each student a card to prepare. When they feel ready to explain their abbreviation, the students should stand up, choose a partner and take it in turns to explain their abbreviation. When the pair has done this, they should exchange cards. The students then move on to find new partners, this time explaining the new word, and so on. If you have fewer than 12 students in the group, feed in new cards to replace ones that everyone has learned. When the activity is over, ask the students to complete the exercise in their course books in writing.

Answers:
a) s = seconds
b) min = minute(s)
c) h/hr = hour(s)
d) g = gram(s)
e) mg = milligram(s)
f) μm = micrometer(s)/micron(s)
g) O = Oxygen
h) MW = molecular weight
i) U = atomic mass unit
j) bp = boiling point
k) DNA = Deoxyribonucleic Acid
l) UV = ultraviolet

Task 3 Using numbers and abbreviations in the *Results* section

3.1 Pairwork
Possible answers:
a) • incorrect punctuation used to express ratios – should use colon, e.g., 2:1
   • inconsistent expression of numbers – should all use decimals to the same number of places, e.g., 3.25.
b) Abbreviations should appear in parentheses after the full name in the title (and the title should appear above the table).
c) Statistics would improve the discussion of the data in the *Results* section.

Unit 5 – The *Discussion, Introduction, Bibliography,* and *Title* sections

At the end of this unit students will know:
• what to include in the *Discussion* section of a report;
• how to cite references and write a bibliography;
• how to write an appropriate Title and Introduction.

Task 1 What to include in the *Discussion*

1.1 Small group work
Encourage students to discuss the table of results together and make a note of their questions.

Possible answers:
• Are there any significant differences in overall beetle numbers?
• Are there any significant differences in the numbers of species found?
• Are there any differences in the beetle assemblages?
• Are there more species that are rare/of conservation importance in one wood compared to the other?

1.2 Individual work/pairwork
After students have worked through the exercise individually, ask them to compare answers with a partner.

Answers:
• Explain whether your results support your original <u>hypothesis</u>.
• Consider any surprising data or <u>deviations</u> from what you expected.
• Relate your findings to previous results in the same area and derive <u>conclusions</u> about the process you are studying.
• Look at the practical and theoretical <u>implications</u> of your findings.
• Make <u>suggestions</u> for extensions of your study.

1.3 Individual/pairwork
After students have worked through the exercise individually, ask them to compare answers with a partner. Question b) can be extended by encouraging the students to explain:

- why certain language features appear in the first or second paragraph of the discussion section only;
- the meaning of each modal in context;
- which relative clause is reduced and why;
- why 'that' is used after reporting verbs.

Answers:
a)

Discussion

The results show that populations of common beetle species were similar in both woodlands and were comparable to numbers found in previous studies. These common beetles are found in most woodland habitats and can be described as generalists. As expected, it was also found that the diversity of beetle species was higher in Pound Wood than in West Wood. Pound Wood was found to contain a surprisingly high number of beetle species which are rare in the UK and which can be described as specialists.

The results show that, for beetles, Pound Wood is of more conservation interest than West Wood. It is a suitable habitat for some beetle species that are rare in Britain and are the subject of species recovery plans that aim to increase their numbers in UK habitats. Pound Wood, therefore, should take priority in management and investment for beetle conservation purposes over West Wood. However, this data says nothing of the overall biodiversity of either of the woodlands. There may be other species of conservation importance present in West Wood that have not been recorded in this study. Therefore, further work should be carried out to assess the overall biodiversity of both of these woodlands before any decisions regarding management or investment are made for either.

b) The passive[1], the past tense[2], comparative structures[3], modal verbs[4], relative clauses[5] (with head noun in box) are all used, but the imperative is not.

Discussion
The results show that populations of common beetle species were similar in both woodlands and

were comparable to **numbers** (that were) found in previous studies[3][2][5]. These common beetles are found[1] in most woodland habitats and can be described[4][1] as generalists. As (it was) expected[2][1], it was also found[2][1] that the diversity of beetle species was higher in Pound Wood than in West Wood[3][2]. Pound Wood was found[2][1] to contain **a surprisingly high number of beetle species** which are rare in the UK[5] and which can be described as specialists[5][4][5].

The results show that, for beetles, Pound Wood is of more conservation interest than West Wood[3]. It is a suitable habitat for **some beetle species** that are rare in Britain[5] and (that) are the subject of **species recovery plans** that aim to increase their numbers in UK habitats[5]. Pound Wood therefore should[4] take priority in management and investment for beetle conservation purposes over West Wood. However, this data says nothing of the overall biodiversity of either of the woodlands. There may[4] be **other species of conservation importance** (that are) present[5] in West Wood that have not been recorded in this study[5][1]. Therefore, further work should be carried[4][1] out to assess the overall biodiversity of both of these woodlands before any decisions regarding management or investment are made[1] for either.

Task 2 Citing references and writing a bibliography

2.1 Individual work/pairwork
Ask students to work individually to work out the order of information rule. Ask them to compare their answer with their partner's.

Answer:
Family Name, Initial(s) (Year of publication). *Title, edition if not first one*. City of publication: publisher.

Southwood, T.R.E. (1984). *Ecological Methods with Particular Reference to the Study of Insect Populations, 2nd ed*. New York: Chapman and Hall.

2.2 & 2.3 Individual work/pairwork
Ask students to work through the questions individually and then to compare their answers with their partner's.

Answers:
a) *Eur. J. Neurosci.*: 13 (1), 2025–2036
   13 = volume number
   (1) = issue number
   2025–2036 = page numbers

b) NMDA
   Eur. J. Neurosci.

c) The first reference is to an article in an electronic journal while the second one is to one in a printed journal.

Task 3 What to include in the *Introduction*

3.1 Small group work
Ask students to discuss which questions are addressed in the *Introduction*.

Answers: b) & c)

3.2 Small group work
Get students to reorganise the sentences to make an introductory text. There is a photocopiable activity on the following page. If you use this, encourage students to explain how the underlined phrases help to link the different parts/ideas of the *Introduction* together.

Answers:
   b), e), d), a), c), f)

Review the task by eliciting from students a likely order of information.
A suggested answer is:
1 Start with a general statement relating to the topic under investigation.
2 Move on to the specific focus of the study.
3 Provide background information from the literature (cite references).
4 Identify unanswered questions or inconsistencies.
5 State the aim and objectives of the current study.

Text to reorder (photocopiable):

a) <u>Many of these species</u> are the subject of species recovery plans designed to manage suitable habitat and increase their numbers. Organisations with responsibilities for areas of woodlands are often lacking in sufficient resources to protect the entire woodland habitat under their jurisdiction.

b) Woodland habitats have been in decline throughout Britain for centuries. This decline has been most notable since the Industrial Revolution and the mechanisation of farming practices.

c) <u>Therefore, they</u> have to prioritise woodlands that are in need of immediate protection.

d) <u>The organisms</u> under most threat are the plants and the insects. These organisms tend to have low dispersal rates and are slow to colonise new habitats. Many species of plants and invertebrates are now threatened with extinction in Britain due to a loss of habitat.

e) <u>With the decline in woodland</u>, many organisms are under threat from a loss of habitat.

f) This study assesses the importance of two woodland habitats to beetle conservation.

Task 4 What makes a good *Title*?

4.1 & 4.2 Small group work/plenary

After the students have discussed which title is better and why in small groups, collect ideas together as a class.

Answer:

Title 2: The effect of temperature on oxygen consumption in mice

The second title is better because it gives the reader a more complete description of the study. The first is too general; the second includes important key words and phrases (temperature, oxygen consumption, mice).

4.3 Pairwork

Ask pairs of students to discuss this question. Ask them to write down, in note form, their conclusions about what makes a title appropriate. Encourage pairs to feed back to the class.

Answers:

Title 1: Species composition of summer phytoplankton in Lake Windermere, Great Britain

Title 1 provides the required information, including key words and phrases (summer phytoplankton; Lake Windermere).

Title 2: Morphological and ultrastructural effects of sublethal cadmium poisoning on Daphnia species

Title 2 provides the required information, including key words and phrases.

Ask students to bring a corrected piece of their scientific writing to the next class.

Unit 6 – Editing and revising your report

At the end of this unit students will be more aware of how to:

- check work for grammatical and vocabulary mistakes;
- edit work to ensure they use full sentences that are clear and concise.

Ask students to bring a corrected piece of their scientific writing to this class.

Task 1 What do I check for?

As a lead-in, focus students on the visual and elicit what correction needs to be made and what 'sp' stands for.

1.1 Small group work

Ask students to predict which problem areas will cause tutors most problems and which they feel are difficult for them personally.

1.2 Individual work

Ask students to use the piece of writing they have brought to class and to work through the questions in Exercise 1.1. This should help them to categorise their errors. They should then count the number of errors of each type in order to identify the areas of writing that are most problematic for them.

Answers will vary, but the following are common problem areas:

1 correct use of tenses
2 correct punctuation
3 correct spelling
4 correct terminology
5 correct grammar
6 clarity
7 numbers
8 abbreviations

Task 2 Use of tenses

2.1 & 2.2 Individual work/pairwork
Ask students to work through the exercises individually and then check their answers to Exercise 2.1 by looking back through the previous units in the course book, before discussing their answers in pairs.

Answers:
2.1

a) was   d) varied
b) presents   e) found
c) is   f) is; results

2.2

Sentence a) uses the passive as in the *Materials and Methods* section. Who did an action is unimportant information. The focus is on what happened.

Task 3 Common mistakes with vocabulary

3.1 Individual work/pairwork
This exercise could be copied onto OHT and initially completed as a team competition before students complete the exercise in the book.

Answers:
a) 1) affects
   2) effects
b) 1) continuous
   2) continual
c) 1) cites
   2) site
d) 1) there
   2) their

3.2 Individual work
Elicit the differences between the pairs of words before students start writing their pairs of sentences.

a) Fewer + countable noun / less + uncountable noun
b) breath = noun / breathe = verb
c) rise = intransitive verb / raise = transitive verb
d) consecutive = one after another without interruption / concurrent = happening at the same time

3.3 Pairwork
Students compare answers. Students' sample sentences could be collected together on the board and then the class could vote for the best ones.

Task 4 Plurals

4.1 Group work
This exercise could be copied onto OHT and initially completed as a team competition before students complete the exercise in the book.

Answers:

Singular	Plural
analysis	analyses
bacterium	bacteria
criterion	criteria
datum	data*
formula	formulae/formulas
hypothesis	hypotheses
medium	media
ratio	ratios
phenomenon	phenomena

Note: You might like to draw students' attention to 'data', which was a plural form traditionally, but can be used as a singular.

4.2 Individual work
Answers:
a) Greek or Latin-based singular nouns that end in ~*um* generally form the plural by changing ~*um* to ~*a*.
b) Greek or Latin-based singular nouns that end in ~*is* generally form the plural by changing ~*is* to ~*es*.

4.3 Individual work
Ask students to underline the subject head noun in each sentence before they check the number in the verb.

Answers:
a) This data* is / These data are supported by evidence from other studies.
b) Ten drops of hydrochloric acid were added to each sample.
c) The period of immersion for crabs at different times of the tidal cycle are **is** presented in Table 1.

d) One <u>source</u> of error in these experiments ~~are~~
   is the inaccuracy in recording light intensities.

Task 5 Be clear and concise

5.1 Pairwork/small group work
Answers:
   a) The zooplankton were affected by pH.
   b) The experiments alone cannot indicate the
      optimum conditions.
   c) 50ml aliquots 0%, 5%, 10%, 15%, 20%,
      25%, 30%, 35%, 40%, 45% sodium chloride
      solutions were placed in test tubes.

Task 6 Write in complete
sentences

6.1 Pairwork/small group work
Answers:
   a) In the third set of experiments, citric acid
      concentration was doubled and at each
      temperature three sets of readings.
      *In the third set of experiments, the
      concentration of citric acid was doubled and
      three sets of readings were taken at each
      temperature.*
   b) Enzymes are denatured at high temperatures.
      Because molecular conformation is altered.
      *Enzymes are denatured at high temperatures
      because molecular conformation is altered.*
   c) The reaction occurred at its maximum;
      copper was absent.
      *The reaction occurred at its maximum when
      copper was absent.*

Abbreviations Snowball

s = second(s)	O = Oxygen
min = minute(s)	MW = Molecular Weight
h/hr = hour(s)	U = atomic mass unit
g = gram(s)	bp = boiling point
mg = milligram(s)	DNA = Deoxyribonucleic Acid
μm = micrometer(s)/micron(s)	UV = Ultraviolet

10 Research and Referencing

Introduction

Preparation for this module

In this module students develop their research and referencing skills by 'improving' an essay on the issue of homelessness, which lacks substantiation and referencing. The module requires students to research the topic, identify relevant sources and select appropriate material to include in their improved essays. If, in your teaching setting, access to an English-language academic library is not possible, you might want to source English-language books and articles on the topic in advance and make a mini-reference library for your students to use, as it is important that they learn to use and reference books and journal articles as well as Internet sources.

Unit 1 – Why research?

At the end of this unit students will:
* understand the need to refer to other sources;
* be able to strengthen the argument in their essays using supporting points and evidence.

Task 1 Why research?

1.1 Small group work

Your role is that of facilitating a group discussion. Lead in by drawing the students' attention to the various photos and asking them if they match the students' definitions of homelessness. You could ensure that students discuss the topics by moving from group to group and, where necessary, introducing the questions.

1.2 Plenary

You could conclude the plenary discussion by pointing out that, without research, an essay relies on the 'common sense' knowledge of the student. This often results in a limited argument or a mistruth. If appropriate, you could elicit what happened when Copernicus and Galileo claimed that the Earth revolved around the Sun.
Alternatively, you could set this as a research task.

Task 2 Supporting evidence and arguments

2.1 Individual work

Depending on the level of the students, the following vocabulary may need to be pre-taught:

homelessness;	*a root cause;*
to have a negative/positive impact;	*a symptom;*
	to target (a problem);
to have a (profound) effect;	*a problem will be*
to address a problem;	*perpetuated;*
a pressing/urgent problem;	*the severity of its impact.*
to have access to;	
adequate housing;	
affordable housing;	
to be impaired;	
domestic violence;	
social integration;	

Answers:
  a) Not given – note: the text says homelessness is a 'pressing' and 'urgent' problem, but no facts or figures are supplied to substantiate the size of the problem.
  b) Poverty, a lack of employment, a shortage of affordable housing, domestic violence, mental illness and drug addiction. (paragraph 3)
  c) A negative impact on physical and mental health, sense of identity and social integration. In the case of homeless children, academic performance may be impaired as well. (paragraph 4)
  d) Only if its root causes can be targeted. (final paragraph)

2.2 Small group work

Lead in by explaining that a tutor evaluating this essay would have to use a set of criteria to do this. Elicit from the students what criteria they would expect the tutor to use and collect the students' ideas on the board. Then set Exercise 2.2.

2.3 Individual work/pairwork

If your group finds this task difficult, you may need to hold a plenary session in which you identify claims made in the essay and check if there is any substantiation provided for the claims.

Task 3 Academic cultures

Individual work/pairwork
Depending on the level of the students, the following vocabulary may need to be pre-taught:
bibliography;
quotation;
in-text reference.

It is useful to bring some academic books to class and ask students to find a bibliography and an index and to ask how the two differ. It is also useful to ask students to find examples of in-text references and to elicit which name is given and what this family name and date indicate. You could also ask them to find examples of quotations and citations. These ideas will be returned to in Units 3 and 4 so it can be useful to establish some familarity with them early on.

Unit 2 – The research process

At the end of this unit students will be:
- aware of a range of sources of information;
- able to identify the strengths and weaknesses of different sources;
- able to note down bibliographical details for books and Internet sites.

If possible, hold this lesson in a teaching room in or close to the library.

Task 1 Research options

1.1 Small group work
Depending on your students' needs, it might be a good idea to take them on a tour of an academic library if this is feasible, in order to show them the many different possible sources of information. Alternatively, examples of different sources of information could be brought to the classroom and students could be asked what they all have in common.

Possible answers include:
  newspapers
  conference papers
  theses
  electronic journals
  television programmes
  films and videos
  online images

1.2 Small group work
You may need to pre-teach:
authority;
ease of access;
reliability.

You might need to fill in any gaps missed by the students, e.g., websites may not be as authoritative as authored books or refereed journals, some sources may be biased etc. You could point out that http://www.rdn.ac.uk/ is a useful website for students to visit in order to learn how to evaluate websites on their particular academic subject. This site gives help in judging the authority and possible bias of sources.

Depending on the needs and abilities of your students, you might like to consider using the following article with your students to stimulate discussion about websites:
Grassian, E. (2000) *Thinking critically about World Wide Web resources* [online]. Available from: <http://www.library.ucla.edu/libraries/college/help/critical/index.htm>

Task 2 Preparing research questions

2.1 & 2.2 Small group work
Ask students to work together in the same small groups as for Unit 1 to compile a list of useful information. They should then turn all the items on their list into research items together. They should then divide up the items equally between the group members and then complete the research question section of the three tables with their allotted items.

Task 3 Information for a bibliography

3.1 Individual work/pairwork
You may need to pre-teach:
full name;
edition;
publication;
publisher.

Answers:
- a) James Smythe
- b) 2004
- c) The Homeless Problem
- d) Second
- e) London
- f) University of Lonbridge Press

3.2 Individual work/pairwork
You may need to pre-teach:
to update information;
to access a website.

Answers:
- a) Frances Martin
- b) 19 September 2005
- c) Homelessness: a perpetual problem
- d) http://www.dailyinformer.com/news/rb_43129

Task 4 Researching

4.1 & 4.2 Individual work/pairwork
Lead in by focusing students' attention on the visual. Explain that a student is trying to find out some information on homelessness and this is what his/her Internet search returned. Elicit what went wrong.

Send students off in pairs to do Exercises 4.1 and 4.2 or set these tasks for homework. Encourage students to make photocopies of relevant parts of the sources they find, to download texts or to borrow the source books where possible. Tell the students that they should bring these sources to class when they have lessons on this module, e.g., see Unit 4.

The exercises in Task 4 need to be marked carefully before you proceed to the next unit, as this will tell you where your students are having problems with collecting bibliographical information. You may need to recycle some of Unit 2 before moving on.

Unit 3 – Writing a bibliography

At the end of this unit the students will:
- understand the purpose of a bibliography;
- be able to produce a bibliography using the Harvard system.

This unit asks students to complete a practical exercise and compile a bibliography. This will involve private study time, both in the library and on the Internet. The bibliography needs checking so that students receive feedback on any inaccuracies.

Task 1 Why include a bibliography?

1.1 Small group work
Possible answers:
- a) This depends on individual student's experiences.
- b) A bibliography is useful for the reader as it provides the reader (the marker) with a record of your research. It allows the reader to verify information given in your writing and it allows the reader to research into the area by pointing him/her in the direction of useful sources.
- c) Writing a bibliography is useful for the student writer because it makes him/her aware of previous scholarship on the topic. It acts as a record of the student writer's research and is useful for revision purposes. It is a behaviour that makes him/her part of his/her academic community.

1.2 Small group work
Possible answers:
- a) It is hoped that your students used the bibliographies to identify more relevant sources. Also, if they noticed that certain authors or texts appeared in many bibliographies, the students might have guessed that these carry some authority on the topic.
- b) If information is missing from the bibliography, a student writer runs the risk of being accused of plagiarism and thus being firmly placed outside his or her academic community. If the information is inaccurate, a student writer runs the risk of being considered lazy or incompetent. Not observing the conventions of referencing might also place the student outside his or her academic community in some tutors' eyes.

Task 2 Bibliographies and the APA system

2.1, 2.2 & 2.3 Individual work

Answers to 2.1:
a) *Homelessness: what's the problem?*
b) 1990
c) Blackwell
d) 2nd edition – i.e., the text of the second edition is not the same as that of the first edition
e) Edinburgh
f) *Housing and social inequality*
g) They refer to books published in the same year by the same author(s)
h) Family name, initial. & Family name, initial.
i) The name of the organisation, government department, etc.
j) In alphabetical order

It is worth checking through the answers and clarifying any areas that confuse your students. It might be worth clarifying, for example, the difference between an edition and a reprint/re-impression, since students often confuse the two when they take bibliographical information from the publishing details page.

You might like to consider explaining that if a name appears with a comma in the middle, this indicates that the family name has been given first, e.g., Bryer, David.

Also, students might find it useful to make a note of a writer's full first name(s), even though an initial is all that is given in the bibliography. This is because the student might need to know whether a writer is male or female when referring to him/her in a piece of writing. When checking an author's sex, this website is useful:
http://www.babynamesworld.com/

Task 3 Bibliographies and electronic sources

3.1, 3.2 & 3.3 Individual work

Answers to 3.1:
a) 2000
b) 24 October, 2006
c) It has a corporate author.
d) 2005
e) It has '.edu' in its web address. This suggests that it is an educational institution. '.ac' is a similar indicator
f) No date is given.

3.4 Group work

Answers:
a) You include the date you accessed a website in a bibliography as websites are frequently updated. Unlike books with their clearly labelled number of editions, it is harder to trace changes made to a website.
b) Depends on the websites selected by individual students.

In a plenary, elicit from students ways of establishing the reliability of a website.

Remind your students to bring their photocopies, downloaded copies or borrowed copies of source texts to the lesson on Unit 4.

Unit 4 – Referring to other sources in your essay

At the end of this unit students will:
- understand how to decide between citing and quoting;
- be able to cite and quote;
- be able to acknowledge their sources in the body of their essays.

Task 1 Citing

Lead in by focusing your students' attention on the visuals. Revise the principle of previous scholarship use by asking your group why students need to refer to what other people have said or written. Then ask what the benefit of making notes is, as opposed to using a highlighter on a photocopy.

It is probably worth emphasising the importance of note-taking as a way of understanding an argument

as well as of avoiding the trap of unintentional plagiarism.

1.1 Pairwork
Answers:
a) Many students probably feel that they share this idea.
b) To add authority.
c) By stating Grassian's family name.
d) Although an initial is given in the bibliography, it is not necessary in the in-text acknowledgement unless the writer is using two sources written by authors with the same family name but not the same initial in a piece of writing.
e) By giving the author's name and date in brackets both of which point the reader to the title of the website, etc., in the bibliography.
f) A combination of changing the word forms 'not all [x] are equally' ? [x] vary; changing the order of ideas 'valuable or reliable' ? accuracy and usefulness & using synonyms 'valuable' ? usefulness.

1.2 Small group work
It might be useful to suggest to students that they word-process a 'working' bibliography before they start drafting their essay. In this way, it is relatively easy to add in-text acknowledgements accurately and quickly.

Task 2 Quoting

2.1 Pairwork
Lead in by focusing your students' attention on the visuals and elicit what 'quoting' is. Ask the students to read through the explanation individually to find out:
- why academic writers generally tend to cite more than they quote;
- an example of when quoting is preferable to citing.

Then ask the students to discuss the questions in Exercise 2.1 in pairs.

Answers:
a) Possibly because this homeless person's words are so direct and provide a strong contrast with the government definition of homelessness.
b) 'I think I was homeless, not because I was living in the street, basically because we, me and my sister, were living at a different house every week and basically living out of a bag in that house.'
c) 'A number of studies (Anderson and Thompson 2005; Fitzpatrick 2000) have found that young homeless people's definitions of homelessness differ from the definition used by the government, which is discussed above. One interviewee says,'
d) Use of inverted commas and the in-text reference.
e) To indicate to the reader which specific text written by Anderson and Thompson to look for in the bibliography.
f) Page 21. The page number is included as a specific part of a source text has been referred to rather than the whole text.

2.2 Pairwork
Answers:
a) Their overview is co-published by the Joseph Rowntree Foundation, one of the leading charities in the area of homelessness and social policy.
b) *Et alia* = 'and others', and is used when a text is co-authored by three or more authors.
c) It means that the writer who is quoting has omitted material from the source text.

2.3 Pairwork
Focus the group's attention on the Shelter logo and elicit what this organisation does. Depending on the level of the students, the following vocabulary may need to be pre-taught:
to accept s.o. as [adj.];
record numbers of;
to be trapped in a place;
temporary accommodation;
overcrowded housing;
unfit housing;
to give s.o. a misleading impression.

Answers:
a) A long quotation is indented, has no quotation marks and is often single-spaced.
b) There is no official maximum, but it is better to avoid lengthy quotations in the body of an essay. These may be put in an appendix if necessary.
c) When the material is taken from a source with no page numbers – a website in the example given.

2.4 Small group work

Answers:

a) The first is a quotation whereas the second is a citation.

b) Citing is usually preferable to quoting as, if done well, it shows the tutor that a student has understood the source material.

c) The tutor's view may be that such a technique does not allow the student to demonstrate his or her ability to understand or use appropriately the ideas of others. If the student does not comment on the whole of a lengthy quotation, the tutor may feel that the quotation was simply 'padding' – words used to reach a word count – rather than contributing to the meaning of the essay.

d) If a student misrepresents a source writer's ideas or opinions in his or her writing, the tutor may view this as evidence that the student has not understood the source material.

e) Accusations of plagiarism may be made.

Task 3 Citing and quoting practice

3.1 Individual work

Ask students to use their library copies, downloaded copies and/or photocopies of source texts for this activity. Although this task needs checking by the teacher eventually, make sure peer evaluation (Exercise 3.2) takes place first.

3.2 Pairwork

Your role is to support this activity. Many students find peer evaluation daunting. You might like to pre-teach some appropriately indirect language first, e.g.:

- Maybe the meaning of the original text has changed a little bit in the paraphrase because …
- Isn't this paraphrase a little bit too similar to the original as …?
- Could there be a mistake in this in-text reference here?

3.3 Individual work

Before setting the task, elicit the ways in which a quotation could be introduced in an essay, e.g.:

- To quote from [family name(s) of source text writer(s)],
- According to [family name(s) of source text writer(s)],
- In his/her/their book/article, [family name(s) of source text writer(s)] state(s) that …

3.4 Pairwork

Again, your role is to support this activity as many students find peer evaluation daunting.

Task 4 Referencing practice

4.1 Group work

Depending on the needs of the students, the following vocabulary may need to be pre-taught:
the primary cause of sth.;
a claim.

Answers:
Sections that aren't properly referenced are underlined. Explanation is in **(bold brackets)**.

In a recent article on homelessness in London, an expert **(name and date)** analysed the reasons behind the growing numbers of homeless people in the city and concluded that drug abuse was the primary cause of homelessness amongst young people. This claim is, however, questioned by another academic **(name and date)** on the website www.homeless.co.uk. According to the second author, **(name should be given, but it is acceptable to omit the date as this has been included above)** the first author's **(name should be given, but it is acceptable to omit the date as this has been included above)** statement 'drug abuse is common amongst homeless people under the age of 20' is not supported by the statistical evidence provided by the National Statistics bureau **(corporate name and date)**.

Unit 5 – Plagiarism

At the end of this unit students will:
- understand what plagiarism is;
- understand how to use sources in their writing;
- be able to recognise plagiarism in a piece of writing.

Task 1 What is plagiarism?

1.1 Small group work

Possible answers:

a) To show evidence of your research efforts, to provide substantiation and to allow your reader to verify your data.

b) It might be worth pointing out that definitions of plagiarism are not universal and that individual tutors in the same department of the same institution may disagree about its definition or deal with the problem in a different way, ranging from ignoring it to initiating a formal enquiry into the case of suspected plagiarism.

1.2 Small group work

Depending on the needs of the students, the following vocabulary may need to be pre-taught:

a push/pull factor;
vulnerable
interpersonal;
break up;
juvenile;
destitute;
formal/recognised qualification.

Answers:

a) Plagiarism is associated with the concept of 'theft' – theft of ideas/language. (It is considered improper behaviour and may cause the plagiarist to be penalised in some way.) Acceptable reference is seen as proper behaviour, but subject tutors may not feel that it is their role to teach the skill of referencing as tutors often take it for granted that everyone knows how to reference.

b) Tutors take plagiarism seriously because it is considered a type of cheating. The act of plagiarism does not develop any academic skills. Moreover, it does not provide the tutor with accurate evidence of the student's abilities.

c) Yes, due to the ease of cutting and pasting and of obtaining online essay-writing services. Conversely, no, as it is very easy to spot cutting and pasting by 'googling' a string of words.

d) No, a number of native speakers are found guilty of plagiarising each year.

e) Most universities impose a penalty. This may be a severe penalty, e.g., awarding a zero mark for the plagiarised work, or in some cases asking the student to leave the course.

Task 2 Plagiarism and other misuses of sources

2.1 Small group work

Answers:

(a) *Comment:* This version has copied and rearranged the source material and so is clearly plagiarised. Moreover, the Centrepoint acknowledgement is to the wrong information.

(b) *Comment:* The best of a bad bunch, but this version is still quite close to the original.

(c) *Comment:* There is no acknowledgement of Forrester and so this is clearly plagiarised. This version changes the claim in the first sentence by removing the adjective 'youth'. This rewrite was produced by copying the original text and then using a 'synonym' search facility on the computer. The rewrite makes little sense and it does not show much understanding of the source material.

(d) *Comment:* This version acknowledges Forrester's intellectual work: her division of push factors into two categories and her claims regarding the importance of push factors for under-16s and the consequences of such an early and unplanned departure. It also attempts to summarise the main ideas and change Forrester's language. It is therefore not plagiarised. However, Forrester's name is misspelt, no page number is given and the wrong date is given. This version also wrongly attributes Centrepoint's research to Forrester.

Unit 6 – Using supporting arguments

At the end of this unit students will be able to:
- select relevant information from their research notes;
- support their arguments;
- acknowledge their sources acceptably.

Task 1 Using supporting statements

1.1, 1.2, 1.3 & 1.4 Individual work
Before setting the tasks, ask students to work in the same small groups as for Unit 2, Tasks 2 and 4, in order to share the information they discovered in the research phase. Encourage the students to take notes.

You may need to model the process outlined in Exercises 1.1–1.4 so that your students understand the tasks.

1.5 Individual work
This activity could be set for homework. It needs checking.

Task 2 Thinking about the argument

2.1 & 2.2 Small group work
Remind students about using tactful language to disagree with others.

Task 3 Thinking about the research process

3.1 Small group work
Wrap up the session with a plenary in which you facilitate reflection on the aims of the module. Gather student feedback on the board after completion of Task 3. The main point to highlight is the importance of using authoritative sources and supporting evidence in order to substantiate a reasoned argument.

The students' advice for other students starting this module could be collected on a poster for wall display.

Presentations

Introduction

This module takes students step-by-step through the process of preparing and giving a group presentation. At the beginning of the module, set a group presentation task for the class and give the date on which the presentations will be given. Hand out a brief written outline of the task, a list of the assessment criteria and referencing guidelines for the bibliography at this point and ask students to keep this information to hand as it will be used in some of the lessons.

Unit 1 – About presentations

At the end of this unit students will be able to:
- recognise what makes a good presentation;
- understand the process of preparing a presentation.

Task 1 What makes a good presentation?

Lead in by focusing students on the visual and eliciting whether the presentation is formal or informal. Ask students to speculate on how large the audience is and how well the audience knows the speaker.

1.1 Small group work

Students should draw on their own experiences. Your role is to facilitate discussion. Encourage the groups to make notes.

Possible answers could include:
a) interesting topic for the audience, evidence of thorough research, good organisation, explanation of technical terms, clear presentation, good use of eye contact and body language, interesting visuals, use of appropriate vocabulary and grammar.
b) boring topic for the audience, inappropriate content for audience, disorganised, speaking voice too quiet/loud, not enough eye contact, speaking speed too fast or too slow, language inaccuracy, lack of acknowledgement of sources used.

Alternatively, direct students to listen to a presentation and take notes. Give an outstandingly poor short presentation and then set Exercise 1.1b. Ask the groups to then work on Exercise 1.1a.

1.2 Pairwork

Ask the students to close their course books to work on this task. Your role is to facilitate discussion. If you think your students will struggle, provide the steps and ask the students to put them in order.
See the check list in Task 2 for answers.

Task 2 Planning check list

Tell the students to look carefully at the check list in Task 2 and compare with the one they made in Exercise 1.2. As they work, encourage the students to think about any differences; why they wrote alternative or inappropriate steps, or why they omitted certain stages.

On completion, discuss any findings or queries as a class.

Task 3 Grading criteria

3.1 Small group work

Lead in by asking your group what aspects or criteria their teachers used to mark their presentations. Elicit whether the students used these criteria to plan their previous presentation(s). If the students get stuck, direct their attention to the visual in Exercise 3.1 and the planning check list in Task 2.

Possible criteria include:
Teamwork: material well divided between group, evidence of group practice
Research: evidence of research, appropriate choice of sources
Content: appropriate material – amount, level
Argumentation: clear research focus, good selection of ideas and evidence

Organisation: well-planned, clear structure, logical sequence
Clarity of communication: clear explanations of technical terms, clear pronunciation
Language accuracy: appropriate vocabulary and structure
Visual aids: used to support message
Academic requirements: appropriate register, acknowledgement of sources

Unit 2 – Group presentations

At the end of this unit students will:
• understand how to organise the preparation process;
• have a clear idea about individual roles and responsibilities.

The outcome of Module 11 is a group presentation. As Unit 2 introduces the notion of a group presentation, it might be useful to either ask students to choose their own groups or for you to allocate students to groups during this lesson. Each group should select a topic, brainstorm ideas, find a focus and then agree a research question before the end of the lesson. The group should then carry out an initial research phase before moving on to Unit 3. You might like to ask your students to keep a presentation diary in which they detail the steps they took to prepare for the presentation, along with their responses to the reflection questions set at the end of each unit.

Task 1 Advantages and disadvantages

Small group work
Possible answers might include:
  a) advantages:
    • can learn from one another;
    • can share ideas;
    • can develop leadership and/or team-working skills.
  b) disadvantages:
    • organising a group of people can take time;
    • weaker members might avoid work;
    • possibility of one or more strong members dominating.

Tasks 2, 3 & 4 Working together/Group work/Sharing responsibilities

Presentation group
Lead in by focusing your group's attention on the visual and asking what point is being made.

These tasks require the students to focus on time and people management skills. If your students are keeping a presentation diary you could ask them to keep a record of meeting information (Table 3.1) and an attendance record (Table 3.2) in their diaries, as well as notes from each meeting of what was discussed and agreed. They should also keep a record of the distribution of tasks among members of the presentation group (see table on course book page 8).

Unit 3 – Content

At the end of this unit students will:
• understand how to prepare and organise a presentation.

Task 1 A short presentation

Before starting on Unit 3, members of the group should be encouraged to share their research with the other group members by giving brief presentations within their groups. Members can then take notes on both content and the speaker's presentation skills. The groups should be encouraged to participate in peer evaluation of presentation skills. This peer feedback could be recorded in the presentation diaries.

The groups should be encouraged to make a note of all sources used so that an accurate bibliography can be produced at a later date.

1.1, 1.2 & 1.3 Presentation group/pairwork
Ask the groups to think about the feedback they gave and received within their presentation groups when they exchanged their research, and to use this experience to help them think of ideas.

1.4 Presentation group
Encourage the students to keep their presentations brief, giving an explanation or supporting point for each main point.

1.5 Plenary

Encourage students to share both good and bad points.

Task 2 Introduction to planning

2.1 Individual work/plenary

Invite a few students to explain what the diagram means, e.g., say what you are going to say; say it; say what you have said. Elicit from the students what a speaker might do in the introductory section (e.g., welcome the audience, introduce him/herself, introduce the topic, give the listener a reason for listening, outline the main sections of the presentation), and in the conclusion (e.g., give a summary of the main points, emphasise the most important points, point to how the topic might be developed in the future, etc.).

2.2 Presentation group

Groups should be encouraged to use this activity to discover how much the rest of the class already knows about the topic and its technical language, and which areas of the topic are of particular interest to other class members. This feedback could be recorded in the presentation diaries and used at a planning meeting.

Tasks 3 & 4 Planning your presentation/ Preparing notes

Presentation group

These tasks could be set for homework. If students need help with the form the bibliography should take, refer them to *TASK* Module 10: *Research and Referencing.*

If students find the idea of presenting from anything other than a full script (either memorised or actual) unrealistic or too challenging, it might be worthwhile reflecting back on Exercise 1 and asking the students to explain what some of the dangers of memorising or reading aloud a script might be.

Possible dangers might include:
Memorising: the speaker looks to the left all the time, rather than the audience, which is common when people are remembering; the speaker comes to a grinding halt when he/she cannot remember the next part.

Reading aloud: the speaker's voice is monotonous; he/she drops her/his notes and cannot find her/his place again; he/she looks at the notes throughout.
Dangers common to both memorising *and* reading aloud: the speaker is unable to summarise easily the remaining part of the talk when he/she runs out of time and so speeds up; the act of writing a text makes the speaker tend towards more formal language, e.g., long and complex sentences, arcane vocabulary.

In preparation for Unit 4, ask students to prepare a three-minute presentation on a topic of their choice, making keyword or bullet-point notes only.

Unit 4 – Communication

At the end of this unit students will:
- be more familiar with the language of presentations;
- be able to use appropriate body language.

Task 1 The language of presentations

1.1 & 1.2 Individual work

Lead in by eliciting the purpose of signposts on a road. Focus the group's attention on the examples of language in Exercise 1.1 and elicit the similarity between these phrases used accurately in a presentation and the roadside signpost.

Answers:

a)	2	f)	6
b)	4	g)	8
c)	3	h)	9
d)	5	i)	10
e)	1	j)	7

To help your students make this language automatic for them, elicit examples for the different functions and drill pronunciation of the target language with them. Then ask the students to test each other. Divide the group into AB pairs. Student A gives a function listed in Exercise 1.1 at random, e.g., outlining what you are going to say; Student B provides a possible signpost, e.g., 'My presentation today concerns …'. When Student A has covered each function a couple of times, the students swap roles. This approach could be repeated for the language in Exercise 1.2.

If you have asked your students to prepare a short presentation, ask them to work in small groups, taking it in turns to give their presentations and using signposting language where appropriate. One student in the group should monitor for the signposting language used by the speaker, while the other(s) should form the audience. After the presenter has finished speaking, his/her peers should give feedback using the criteria you will use for the assessment of the final presentation.

Task 2 Delivering a presentation

2.1 Pairwork
Possible answers:

smile at the audience: seems welcoming, confident and friendly.

sit down: could make the speaker seem disinterested and make him/her harder to hear.

walk around: this could be distracting; however, measured movement can look purposeful.

look only at notes: makes it hard to hear the speaker, and will make his/her delivery less interesting.

use hand gestures: can create interest and add emphasis.

play with hair/change in pocket/earring, etc.: can be distracting.

lean against a wall: can make the speaker seem disinterested.

point at the audience: might seem aggressive.

2.2 Small group work
To lead in, focus the group's attention on the visuals and ask why the gestures shown might result in a misunderstanding.

Ask the students to jot down brief notes of the group's discussion and to write these up. If you have asked your students to keep a diary, you could ask them to include the piece of writing in this.

Unit 5 – Visual aids

At the end of this unit students will be:
- more familiar with a range of appropriate visual aids;
- able to use visual aids effectively.

Task 1 Choosing and using visual aids

1.1 Pairwork
Some possible answers are:

Visual aid	Advantages	Disadvantages
Posters	a lot of information in one place	time-consuming to prepare and can be difficult for the audience to read
Overhead transparencies	easy and reliable	might seem old-fashioned
Videos	visually appealing and may contain a lot of information	the speaker cannot speak at the same time
Whiteboard	no preparation required	writing takes time and usually requires the speaker to turn his/her back on the audience
Printed handouts	can provide a useful summary to take away	audience might read the handout instead of listening to the presenter
PowerPoint slides	looks professional	may be time-consuming to prepare; Computer problems can cause difficulties

1.2 Pairwork/small group work
Possible answers:
 DON'T:

- crowd too much information into one visual. **It can make the visual difficult to read.**
- put unimportant details in the visual. **These can be distracting and confusing.**
- forget to talk about information in a visual. **It shows poor organisation and may be confusing.**
- use 12-point font or less. **It is likely to be difficult to read.**
- put visuals in a different order to that of information in the presentation. **It will confuse the audience and is evidence of poor preparation.**

Task 2 Preparation of visual aids

Small group work
Lead in by showing some examples of presentation posters to the class. Ask the students to read through the seven questions and answers about presentation posters listed in Task 2 and then invite students to discuss in groups which poster they prefer and why. Then ask the groups to discuss and write down the criteria they used to evaluate the posters.

2.1 & 2.2 Pairwork & small group work
You might prefer to allot a type of visual aid to each pair, possibly providing a couple of examples of the type created by previous students.

Unit 6 – Slideshow tutorial

At the end of this unit students will be able to:

- make a slideshow;
- understand how a slideshow can help get the message across.

This unit could be set as a self-study task. If you choose to do this, it is worthwhile pointing out the importance of using keywords and brief summaries on slides. Integrate some practice of this into a lesson, before setting the unit as a self-study task. Alternatively, within presentation groups, those students who are unfamiliar with PowerPoint could be asked to prepare a slideshow to accompany the

group's presentation, while those who are already proficient in the use of PowerPoint could prepare another type of visual aid, e.g., a poster. The presentation group could then compare the two types of visual aid, looking at their advantages and disadvantages, and then decide which visual aid to use in the group's final presentation.

The students should now be in a position to give their group presentations. Ask students to work in small groups to give feedback to the different presentation groups in writing, possibly using a pro-forma that corresponds, more or less, to the marking criteria you have chosen. Make a copy of the completed peer feedback sheets for each speaker in the group. These can be added to the presentation diaries. Finally, you could ask the individual students to write a short reflective piece on how they have developed their skills as presentation speakers and what areas they would focus on improving in their next presentation.

Unit 1 – Planning for examinations

At the end of this unit students should have:
- a good understanding of their examinations' requirements;
- a revision plan.

This unit has been designed to meet the needs of students who are likely to sit an examination in the fairly near future. If this is the case, you could encourage your students to create a dedicated examination folder in which they collect relevant information about their examination(s), that is to say the outcomes of Exercises 2.2–2.5 in Unit 1. If, however, your students are not sitting an exam in the near future, you might prefer to look at Exercise 1 and Exercise 2.1 in Unit 1 and then move on to Unit 2.

Task 1 The purpose of examinations

1.1 Pairwork
Your role here is to facilitate discussion.

1.2 Small group work
Your role here is to facilitate discussion.

Possible answers:
a) They are a means by which lecturers can check students' understanding.
They are a way of encouraging intensive learning.
b) Intense, short-lived study pressure. They encourage students to develop a good 'map' or overview of a subject.
Less need for perfect presentation of written work.

Task 2 Examination requirements

2.1 Pairwork
If you think your students will struggle with this, it may be useful to have examples of some of the documents mentioned below. You could display the items, or printouts of them, on the classroom wall and ask students to match the descriptions of the documents listed with the realia. Alternatively, show students how to access electronic versions of the information where appropriate.

Possible answers:
a) student handbook
b) departmental website
c) learning outcomes of each module
d) lecture notes provided by tutors
e) past exam papers
f) reading lists
g) comments on coursework

2.2 Individual work
You may need to model this task for your students. The activity lends itself to being a homework assignment, particularly if you ask students to create a special examination folder in which they place copies of the relevant documentation (see Exercise 2.1) and a copy of the table giving key information about their examination(s) (see Exercise 2.2).

2.3 Pairwork
You may need to go round and check your students' work.

Task 3 Exam planner

Individual work
Students need to organise this activity with subject tutors where possible.

Tasks 4 & 5 Revision timetable

Individual work
These activities could be set for homework and then form part of your students' examination folders.

Unit 2 – Memory styles and active learning

At the end of this unit students will:
- understand their personal memory styles better;
- have developed strategies to help themselves to memorise.

Task 1 Your memory style

1.1 Individual work
This exercise is designed to help students focus on the techniques they already use to help themselves memorise information. Techniques might include:

a) visualising a phone (or other) number, or a route
b) singing a number
c) hearing yourself say a number
d) tapping your fingers to the rhythm of a favourite song
e) hearing your favourite song
f) singing the song to yourself
g) tasting/smelling a favourite food
h) remembering the place where you used to eat the food.

1.2 Pairwork
It might be useful to initiate a plenary discussion after the pairwork stage so that the students realise how many different methods could be used to remember the information.

1.3 & 1.4 Individual work/pairwork
The purpose of these activities is to prepare the students for the idea of there being three basic learning styles. They might find that any of the following may have helped them memorise:
- colour awareness: colour to aid memory;
- spatial awareness: where the words are located on the page;
- visual awareness: capitals, underlining etc.;
- sound awareness, e.g., words that start with the same sound;
- order awareness: the words that were learnt first/last;
- meaning awareness, e.g., words that belong to a group (e.g., small, tiny, little).

1.5 Individual work
a) auditory
b) auditory
c) visual
d) visual
e) auditory
f) kinaesthetic
g) visual
h) auditory
i) kinaesthetic/visual

1.6 Pairwork
Ask students to make notes of their discussions as they will have the opportunity to test themselves later in order to gain an insight into their learning styles (see Web work, website 2 at the end of the module).

Task 2 A deeper understanding

2.1 Individual work
You might prefer to use an alternative task to the one in the book. For example, you could bring a picture of an object cut into pieces and give students one piece, telling them to keep it hidden. Ask them to take it in turns to describe their piece and elicit the name of the object. Then ask the group to fit the pieces of the puzzle together to check if their proposed answers were correct.

2.2 Individual work

Concept	Parts
Society	group of people
	particular place
	share a distinctive culture and set of institutions

You could extend this activity by finding a description of a core concept in your students' area of study if they are following the same or a similar discipline. Introductory textbooks and subject-specific keyword guides are good sources. Ask the students to identify the concept and its constituent parts and make notes in a table similar to the one above. If your class is mixed in terms of subject of study, you could have a library-based lesson in which you ask students to identify a core concept, find a relevant description and carry out the note-taking activity. In this case, you should be ready to support your students in the research activity as

they might find it difficult to identify relevant material. If your students have access to a reading list for their future course, they should be encouraged to use material indicated on this list.

Task 3 Organising information into groups

3.1 & 3.2 Individual work
Follow the instructions in the course book.

3.3 Pairwork
You might want to frame this discussion by asking students how they learn vocabulary that they have, for example, encountered in a reading text.

Task 4 Reorganising information into diagrams

4.1 Individual work
Answers:
   a) flow chart
   b) timeline
   c) mind map

4.2 Individual work/pairwork
The rewriting activity lends itself to homework. If you used the extension exercise suggested in Exercise 2.2 of this unit, you could ask students to work with these notes.

In the discussion activity, encourage students to explain their reasons for selecting the diagram form they chose as well as explaining the information contained in the diagram. Encourage students to reflect on which form(s) of diagrammatic note-taking best suit(s) the requirements of their own academic discipline.

Task 5 Reorganising information into summary notes

1.1 & 1.2 Individual/pairwork
As a lead-in to this task, it might be worth pointing out to your students that note-taking from previous scholarship and the use of these notes to write a summary is a very common academic routine. Encourage your group to make a note of the bibliographical details of their source text and to include these in their summary in an acceptable manner (see *TASK Module 10: Research and Referencing* for more information).

In a plenary discussion at the end of the unit, in which you elicit from the group the main points they have learnt, it may be worth drawing students' attention to the fact that teaching another person something is often an extremely good way of checking that you have a good grasp of the subject yourself. This is one reason why they should think about setting up a small study group when they start their academic course.

If you are planning to teach Unit 3 next, encourage your students to find an example of a past exam paper for one of the courses they will study on their future academic programme and bring it to the lesson.

Unit 3 – Revision strategies

At the end of this unit students will:
• be aware of the benefits of active revision;
• have a personal revision strategies toolkit.

Encourage students to find an example of a past exam paper for one of the courses they will study on their future academic programme, bring it to the lesson and, later, store it in their examination preparation folders.

Task 1 Pass or fail

1.1 Individual work/small group work
Possible answers:

Pass	Fail
advance planning	poor organisation
good revision strategies	stress
precise notes	lack of revision
extensive reading	illness

1.2 Pairwork
Encourage students to focus on their preparation for a specific exam they took in the past, rather than talking in general.

Task 2 Identifying examination skills

2.1 & 2.2 Individual work/pairwork
Lead in by eliciting other suggestions for the 'Type of question' column and for the 'Skills practice required' column for the two examples given in the course book. A copy of this work could be put in the students' examination preparation folders.

Possible answers:

Type of question	Skills practice required
Answering questions based on a text	• understanding questions fully; • skimming and scanning; • using time effectively.
Essay writing	• essay planning; • title analysis; • proofreading; • using time effectively.
MCQs	• identifying easy, tricky and impossible; questions; • using time effectively.
Data response	• showing calculations stage by stage; • using time effectively.

Task 3 Active and passive revision

3.1 Individual work/pairwork
Lead in by eliciting from your students possible sources of advice available at university for students who are having problems with revising for an exam. Then ask your group to read the letter, underlining Olena's problems and possibly comparing their ideas with their partner, before they take notes.

3.2 Small group work
As an alternative to the instructions in the book, you could ask pairs of students to prepare to role-play Olena's discussions with an academic adviser at her university.

3.3 Individual work/pairwork
Depending on the preferences of your students, they could write individually or in pairs. This activity could be set for homework.

Answers should include some of the following points:
- spending time in a library is not the key solution to exam success;
- break times should be more evenly divided throughout the day;
- research suggests that it is impossible to concentrate for three hours at a time;
- more breaks are recommended towards the end of the day, but breaks every 15 minutes may be disruptive;
- you need a more evenly distributed timetable of revision;
- choose a location without distractions;
- reading without note-taking will not help to consolidate knowledge;
- any problems with understanding the textbook should have been dealt with at an earlier stage.

In order to encourage your students to develop their evaluation skills, you could make a wall display of all the replies to Olena's letter. Explain that the student newspaper can only publish one reply and that the students, as members of the editorial board, have to make the decision about the best answer. Ask students to work in small groups and encourage them to develop a set of criteria for making their decision before they evaluate the letters. It would be useful to have a plenary session on these criteria before moving on to the evaluation stage. Alternatively, this evaluation stage could be carried out through a pyramid discussion.

Task 4 Reading past papers

4.1 Pairwork
Possible answers include:
- to develop a better understanding of the paper;
- to find out how long the paper is;
- to work out how many questions you will have to answer;
- to note the sort of topics that appear regularly;
- to reduce the likelihood of an unpleasant surprise on the day of the exam.

4.2 Individual work

Stages 1–3 could be done in class with Stage 4 set as homework.

Task 5 Revision toolkit

This activity could be set as homework and a copy of it put in the students' examination preparation folders.

Unit 4 – Understanding the exam paper

At the end of this unit students will:

- have a better understanding of how the question paper is organised;
- be able to follow instructions on question papers more accurately.

Task 1 The question paper cover

Plenary

Use the following questions to check how much information students have identified from the exam cover.

- Is there an answer book?
- Where should the answers be written?
- What equipment is permitted?
- How long does the exam last?
- How much time is allowed for each section?
- How many marks are there for each section?
- What percentage of marks does each section contribute to the final total?
- Should the students use some of the time to complete the front of the answer books?
- Why is a candidate number used rather than the candidate's name?

Task 2 The rubric

Pairwork

Explain to students that the most important factor in completing the exam efficiently is understanding the exam rubric completely and following the instructions exactly.

Answers include:

a) • the total number of questions that should be attempted;
   • instructions regarding which questions can be selected.

b) • answering the wrong number of questions or parts of questions, e.g., all the questions on the paper;
   • not following the instructions regarding the rules for selecting questions, e.g., choosing all questions from Section A.

Task 3 Following instructions

3.1 Individual work

In your lesson planning, be prepared for students either to work through this activity quickly or to spend as long as 15 minutes on it.

3.2 Individual/pairwork

When introducing this activity it is important to stress to the group that the exercise is designed to test students' ability to follow instructions, not to test their knowledge of biology.

Answers:
  Section A:
    • students are only supposed to answer one of the three questions;
    • none of the questions are answered as instructed in the rubrics.
  Section B:
    • only supposed to put one word in each space;
    • supposed o answer all parts.
  Section C:
    • supposed to use chemical symbols for 7-9;
    • supposed to write the full name in 10.

Unit 5 – Understanding exam tasks

At the end of this unit students will:
- have a better understanding of how to answer essay questions;
- be able to maximise their performance on multiple-choice questions.

Task 1 Instruction words

1.1 Individual work

This activity could be organised as presented in the course book. Alternatively, the keywords and explanations could be copied onto small cards and used for a vocabulary snowball activity in which each student has a card. Students move around the room, teaching another student the vocabulary on their card and then swapping cards with their partner. They then teach their word to a new partner, exchange cards, and so on until the whole group has learnt the keywords. Then ask the students to complete the exercise in the course book.

Answers:

comment on: Identify the main issues and give an informed opinion.

contrast: Show how two things are different. Explain the consequences of dissimilarities.

analyse: Examine in detail by dividing up. Identify the main points.

define: Give the precise meaning of a term. This may include explaining what is problematic about defining the term.

compare: Show how two things are similar. Explain the consequences of the similarities.

discuss: Look at the most important aspects of something in a balanced way, i.e., advantages and disadvantages, for and against.

describe: Give the main features, characteristics or events.

evaluate: Assess how important or useful something is. It is likely to include both positive and negative points.

explain: Provide reasons for why something happens, or why something is in a particular state.

examine: Take detailed look at something.

make a case: Put forward an argument either for or against a claim.

interpret: Give the meaning or significance of something.

outline: Give the main ideas or information, without any details.

illustrate: Show what something is like, using examples and/or evidence.

justify: Support a claim with evidence, taking into account opposing views.

trace: Put the steps and stages of a process or event into order.

summarise: Give the main points only, using fewer words than the original.

relate: Give the connections between things.

to what extent: Say how much something is or isn't true.

state: Give just the main points, very clearly.

1.2 Pairwork/plenary
Ask students to compare their answers. In a plenary, write up some questions on the board, omitting the instruction word, and elicit which words might complete the cloze.

1.3 Pairwork/plenary
Lead in by asking students to identify the political event being alluded to in the visual. Ask students to discuss how the change in instruction words results in a change in the task. You could allot each pair an essay title and ask them to discuss what the main sections of their essay would be; then compare ideas in a plenary.

1.4 Pairwork
Answers will vary according to the students' disciplines.

Task 2 Question styles

Pairwork/small group work
You may need to take in a sample exam paper and model this task for your class.

Task 3 Exam essay planning and title analysis

3.1 Plenary
Lead in by asking students if they know (of) anyone who speaks and writes English very fluently and accurately without ever having lived in an English-speaking country.

3.2 Individual work
Answers:
  a) two main parts
  b) Is living in an English-speaking country the best way to learn English?
  c) Is it impossible to learn English without living in an English-speaking environment?
  d) iii) Look at the question in a balanced way.

3.3 Individual work
This could be set for homework.

Model answer:
The term 'anglophone' is frequently used to describe countries where English is spoken as a first language. According to Miller and James (1997, p. 36), studying a language in such a country where English is spoken has many advantages. It is therefore, in many ways, a good idea to study English in an anglophone country. However, in this

essay I will argue that it is not the only way to learn a language and that it may have disadvantages for some students.

Most students in non-English-speaking countries learn English at secondary school and sometimes at university (British Council, 2001). Even though their knowledge of spoken English may be weak, one advantage may be that their knowledge of grammar and the written form of the language is often advanced. This language base is certainly useful when students come to an English-speaking country to perfect the language.

In general, studying the basics of English in the home country is less stressful than learning the language overseas. This is because students living at home do not have to worry about such problems as trying to find accommodation, paying for their studies, living costs and trying to survive in a foreign country where day-to-day living may cause stress.

On the other hand, there are obvious advantages to learning English in an English speaking country. Every day there are opportunities to practise listening to and speaking with native speakers (British Council, 2001). Students can experience the culture first-hand, which is a great help when trying to understand the language. This is especially true if they choose to live with a local family, as exchange students for example. In addition, if students attend a language school full-time, the teachers are likely to be native speakers. In this case, not only will students' speaking and listening improve, but attention can be given to developing reading and writing skills also (Miller and James 1997, p. 25).

To conclude, even though it is preferable to study English in an English-speaking country in order to improve listening and speaking skills in particular, in many instances beginners find that it is easier to gain a basic understanding of the language and its grammar before going to live abroad. This is because they do not have to contend with the additional stress of adapting to a new culture and environment at the same time.

Task 4 Planning and analysis in practice

Individual work/pairwork

Encourage your students to think about how many parts the essay has, what issues should be covered and the nature of the overall task. Refer them to *TASK* Module 8: *Essay Writing* for further help. Alternatively, the task could be set for homework and the plans produced by your students could form the basis of either a tutorial or a peer evaluation of the plan session.

Task 5 Timed essay writing

Individual work

This task could be set for homework.

Task 6 Answering multiple-choice questions

Individual work

Ask students to read through the text and practise this technique on some multiple-choice English-language questions before trying the technique out on a past exam paper relevant to their academic discipline(s).

Unit 6 – Managing exam stress

At the end of this unit students will:
- understand how to manage anxiety while they are revising;
- have a plan for managing their stress on the day of the exam.

Task 1 Begin to take control

Pairwork

Lead in by eliciting what the visuals all have in common. Ask your students if they suffer from exam nerves and, if they do, how they cope with them. Then ask the pairs to review the work they have done in this module so far, selecting any ideas that would help them take control.

Task 2 Taking a positive attitude

2.1 Pairwork
Possible answers might include:
- deal with any pent-up energy by doing an energetic activity, e.g., jogging, dancing, swimming;
- revise with another student so that the process is not so lonely;
- try to stay healthy by eating and sleeping well.

2.2 Pairwork
Encourage pairs to discuss their previous experience of sitting exams when they do this evaluation task.

Task 3 Managing your anxiety

3.1 Individual work/pairwork
Encourage students to underline keywords in the heading and in the brief descriptions of techniques in order to complete this task as rapidly as possible.
Answers:
- a) 4
- b) 5
- c) 2
- d) 3
- e) 1

Task 4 Action points

Individual work/pairwork
The work produced could be used to form a wall display. You could also ask your students to write down their own most important action points and keep this list in the front of their examination files.

If your students have created examination files while completing this module, encourage them to write a short reflection on how they have altered their attitudes to examinations and their examination preparation.